Listen.
Struggle.
Repeat.

Step Up Life with Hearing Loss

Dominique Briscoe

Listen. Struggle. Repeat: Step Up Life with Hearing Loss

Copyright © 2021 by Dominique Briscoe

All rights reserved: This book is protected by the copyright laws of the United States of America. No part of this book may be reproduced in any form or by any means, electronic or mechanical, including photocopying, recording, informational storage or retrieval systems, without written permission by the author, except where permitted by law, for the purpose of review, or where otherwise noted

Disclaimer: The stories, anecdotes, and unpublished examples included herein are based on the author's personal encounters and professional experiences. Many names of individuals and parties have been changed to protect privacy and identity.

Book Editor
Desiree Harris-Bonner – Spiritual Midwife for Emerging Authors
https://www.dhbonner.net/

Cover Design
Dr. Donnisha Davis

Printed in the United States of America

Listen.
Struggle.
Repeat.

This work is dedicated to my daughter, *Christian Dominique:*

When I began this book, I had not realized how much my relationship with you would make me stand in my truth. As in every area of my life, you are always there moving mountains and lighting the way. I could not have written this book without you to sincerely bond with and teach me how great I can be as a mother. Someday, you will be an adult, and you will truly understand and cherish the legacy that we have built together through your kind and graceful ways. Thank you!

... and to my family:

Thank you for believing in me even when I doubted myself. Writing this book has enabled me to see how truly blessed a hearing disabled child is when she is raised in a loving and understanding family. Your presence in my life helps me accept this loss as a part of my entire life journey. Thank you!

"Just for today, allow yourself to embrace all that you are every moment. Know that you are a vessel of light. Allow yourself to release all doubts about your ability, the mistakes of the past, the fear of the future."

–*Iyanla Vanzant*

Table of Contents

Introduction 1

Section 1 – What You Need to Know 8

Self-Knowledge is Self-Power 9

1. My Lesser Hearing Journey... Find Your True Internal Power to Overcome a Hearing Loss 11

2. Get this Elephant out of the Room: Understand What Makes Every Conversation a Success! 37

3. You Can't Soar While Hiding Among the Bushes... Know that It All Starts with Your Own Acceptance of Self! 73

Section 2 – What You Need to Change 104

Change Is Good 105

4. Create Your Self-Awareness Hype... Change How You Relate to Others! 107

5. Bring You're "A" Game... Change How You Relate in Your Workplace! 129

6. Kick Relationship Blues… Change How
   You Relate in Your Personal Relationships!.................163

7. Kick These Six Habits: Change What
   Works Against Your Own Self-Love!..............................199

8. The Three C's of Evolving
   Conversations… Change Your Ability to
   Have Meaningful Conversations!......................................225

Section 3 – What You Can Expect 244

High Expectations Yield High Results 245

9. Build Your New Inner Circle… Expect
   Relationships to Blossom from Here on Out!...............247

Conclusion 285

Endnotes 293

Introduction

AT THE MOMENT, OUR society is in this great era of marveling at "self-help" books. So, if you've purchased this book, then I would be willing to bet enormous amounts of money that you're expecting a huge payoff. You can rest assured that the payoff from reading this book will be absolutely abundant, my friend! Hands down! What you will learn here will open your mind and heart and allow you to continuously evolve, become phenomenal, and ever achieving in your life!

My philosophy is to help others, with a similar hearing loss as mine, always be at their best! Why would you need help being at your best, you might ask? Oh, come on! We are tested all day long. People push our buttons; they get under our skin! Have you ever noticed how some people speak extremely low? Whether it's intentional or not, it doesn't matter. The issue is that it raises doubt within us and encourages self-questioning.

Many thoughts roll through our minds while living with a hearing impairment, but this book will be a great confirmation that you are not alone. It will give you a vast glimpse into the reality of how to live and achieve your greatest dreams. I will start by explaining what you need to know about living with a hearing loss, then I will glide into what you need to change in order to embrace it, and finally, we will finish out the book with what you can expect when you put these fascinating strategies to work in your life!

No, I'm not going to say the annoying "you have to look into your soul and find the answer" gesture. I'll do you one better: I will say receive my experiences, connect with them, and decide from reading this book, that you will always be at your best! If you're hard of hearing or faced with another type of impairment, I encourage you to read and receive your "aha" moments!

I want you to get your divine connection with another (myself) because this experience of connecting with others is something that we simply don't enjoy enough while being hard of hearing. You know there is some truth in that last statement. After everything has been said and done, believe me, you will enjoy it. I promise you. You will laugh with me, and you will be overjoyed with me as I share my moments of triumphs and climb inevitable mountains, all while harboring my intense, and sometimes difficult, hearing loss.

If you do not have a hearing loss, yet you are reading this book, then maybe you desire to become more comfortable with loved ones who are facing hearing loss challenges (a parent, a child, a student, a client, etc.). Just rest assured that this book will help you to understand the views, perceptions, and experiences of those who are hearing deprived. And as loved ones, there is nothing we want more than your understanding! So, kudos to you for taking that step!

There is a global, common concern that is a tad bit confusing for many regular and lesser hearing people. It has to do with exactly how to communicate with us or mediate for us; when to repeat for us and when to hold back; what seems too pushy or what seems unsympathetic. Understanding it from the view of a hard-of-hearing author may be just the buttercream icing on the delicious cake that you need to pull this off successfully.

How do we encourage friends and family to try for us, anyway? These are just a few of many issues to consider when we bring together both the lesser hearing and normal hearing loved ones. As a hearing-impaired author, I hope that this book will intelligently answer many of your questions and lovingly embrace your struggle. I will be putting pen to paper and sharing experiences, some of which you, yourself, may have already encountered before, as well; that will be our connection, then you will begin to see and understand what I mean when I say that you are not alone.

No matter your age or status in life, what I will share will be life-changing and enlightening for you. Why do I say that? Because there are simply not enough of us who struggle with hearing loss, and yet, are willing to step up and lead others who are overwhelmed by their hearing loss. The purchase of this book was your first step in a great direction for yourself. I love writing, and I am so excited to share my experiences with you.

On a serious note, don't lose your spunk, don't compromise your goals, don't struggle with this thing. Embrace it, and wonderful things will happen. While writing this book, I conferred with several people about how to appropriately address those who are hearing-impaired and hard of hearing. I have learned that most of these people preferred a few terms: hearing loss, lesser hearing, hearing struggle, hearing deprived, and so forth, as opposed to hearing disabled and hearing impaired.

Therefore, I will be sure to use only the terms that are acceptable across the board throughout this book. Most of the time, I place "hearing" in a sentence, and behind it, I will describe a decreased state of hearing, such as deprived or loss, which seems less offensive. You get my point.

However, this book is about self-acceptance as well; we cannot control what others speak, and with that in mind, I hope that it will lighten your burden of having to hear "appropriate terms" all of the time. Lighten up… it's just life, and it's all good!

The greatest gift I can receive in writing this book is to convey the importance of always being at your best and helping you do just that. Yes, to help you, who purchased this book, to escape the self-doubt and fear that comes with a hearing loss. At a particular time in my life, it had caused a raging storm within me that you probably can relate to. And even today, I remain astonished by the careless mentality of the people in our present day, and I believe that the era of sympathy and simple human care for those who live with impairments is gone with the wind as if it had never been here. With this in mind, we must set out to plan how we can always be at our best, hard of hearing, and all! We cannot change the world, but we can change ourselves.

Just recently, I stopped to help an elderly woman that was coming out of a store. She was carrying a large glass bowl. After walking her to her car, she thanked me; she was extremely appreciative, as the walk to her car had been much easier. That is the type of person that I know I am, and what I would like to be for you. A burden bearer and a burden sharer - sharing your burden and making your walk easier by finding common ground, giving you the love and encouragement that you will receive in reading this book.

Reason #1 that I give you for reading this book would be to enlighten yourself about your hearing loss. Yes, that's actually one of my life's secrets… book reading. In my childhood, and throughout life, reading has been my escape. Everyone needs to escape, right? Some people escape by sitting on a beach or meditating, others ride motorcycles through the mountains.

For me, the escape happens when I can quiet the room, pull my hearing aids out and enjoy reading and communicating, thinking and dreaming, without the struggle of having to hear others but through the use of my luxurious eyes, free from any loss. If you have read this far, then I think, just maybe, we have this in common; so, come on… let's read. Let's get past this thing together, so that your "awakening" will either shine through—or present itself—once again. I use the metaphor "once again" because my "awakening" had to occur "again" in my life.

I was filled with exuberant confidence as an adolescent and young adult, then a combination of life's happenings and this rude, unjust world came and knocked over my lamp. From there, I had to take time out in my life to make my light shine again. I promise you that knocking over Dominique's lamp will never happen again. My heart, my mind, my spirit, and my physical body will not allow it.

That brings me to Reason #2 for reading this book; to keep you out of the valley of self-doubt and self-questioning. We all practice this dreadful habit, but I want to show you how I overcame this. Just think about how many thoughts there are that run rampant through the average person's mind in a day; now add a difficulty with hearing.

Yes, it can be overwhelming. Obviously, it affects your body, but also your mind, heart (physical and emotional), and spirit; however, we just can't live like that. That's letting our life get the best of us. That's allowing your life to lessen your abilities. Let me encourage you by saying no worries… you've got this!

This leads me to Reason #3 for reading this book! It is the true essence of this book! That is, we are going to use it to build your inner circle, giving you your home-court advantage in any situation or environment. Surrounding yourself with those who care and mediate for you is a great way to expect great things.

These great chances will evolve from the work (reading and applying what you learn in this book) that you put into it. Evaluate who is in your life! Do they contribute to your happiness, or exhaust it? Are they patient enough with your hearing loss, or does it enable that pathetic tendency we have to continually question our own capabilities?

This is a part of this book that will be a self-journey for you. We can walk through this entire book together, but to truly apply what you have learned will take just a tad bit of self-analyzing on your part; here's why. Each of our lives is our own. That, my friend, is the true beauty of life—individuality! But no biggie, no sweat because the connections that we make in this awesome book are going to enrich your spirit, build mental well-being, and show you the much more phenomenal picture of YOU! And that grand picture is (drumroll please!) *learning how to always be at your best.*

That's the BIG IDEA behind this book: Understanding how to present yourself well and gain the respect of others. When you adopt this chain of thoughts from my proven strategies, those crabby people who exhaust your energy and work against your "awakening," I promise you, will be given the boot!

SECTION I

What You Need to Know

Lead Page:
Self-Knowledge is Self-Power

WE READ IT ON billboards everywhere, "Knowledge is Power"—in the libraries, schools, camps, community centers, and such. If you can understand that phrase, then you can surely understand the phrase "Self-knowledge is Self-Power," with the latter being a more worthy cause. Don't you agree that self-knowledge is an extremely worthy cause?

Knowledge of self produces confidence, skills, and motivation; it is even strong enough to produce internal peace. Heck, it produces so many things, that I would barely be able to get through this book if I were to list all of them. Now that we agree on this, why leave something so powerful to chance? Why take the risk of never attaining these wonderful traits because you lack self-knowledge, especially living as lesser hearing? There are just too many occurrences and tests that we walk into every single day.

The beginning portion of this book—within its first three chapters—is going to tell you what you need to know about living with a level of lesser hearing. Do you understand how important interpreting body language is? Do you pursue it, or do you simply look away and refuse to give it a try? Have you truly come to terms with your hearing loss and accepted yourself one hundred percent, or are you still struggling with your "off days"? There is no more excellent time than now to get what you need to know because, as I said earlier, self-knowledge is self-power.

So come, read, and conquer it!

CHAPTER 1

My Lesser Hearing Journey... Find Your True Internal Power to Overcome a Hearing Loss

> *"Life is either a daring adventure, or nothing at all. To keep our faces toward change and behave like free spirits in the presence of fate is strength undefeated."*
> —Helen Keller, Hearing Disabled Author

M Y HEART WAS ON my sleeve, and tears fell like rain showers against my face as my audiologist turned to me with a dismayed look on her face and said, "Dominique, let's take a break from testing for a minute." Stepping out of her audiometric sound booth and walking over to me, my heart pounded. I was completely fearful of the dreadful news that she would soon convey. My hearing level had declined *drastically,* once again.

How in the world was I to function in my life, now, with such a horrible declining level of hearing? I felt as if a big light bulb had switched on inside of my head, finally revealing to me the exact severity of my staggering hearing, which was disheartening. Little did I know that it would have a horrible effect on my life during the next few years. It ate away at my self-esteem, tested my self-love, and it swung me into a deep valley of depression.

At the time, I could not foresee the future to know that I would later be okay—to know that I would find my true internal power to overcome a devastating hearing loss. I would be able to eventually pull myself out of this valley of life. That is what I wish to share with you while writing this book. It is an experience that I cannot allow to go unheard.

Sometimes our mind brings the clouds...

In my life, I have learned that we can sometimes save ourselves from depression and heartbreak by merely understanding the true nature of what we struggle with. Your acceptance of it breeds enriching energy that draws people in. With this acceptance, people begin to say things like "I like her", "she's pretty cool". Yet, although it's a physical disability, most of the battle is emotional. We can save ourselves from these heartbreaking experiences of fear and inadequacy when we parallel our lives to others. That is why I invite you to take note of the skills that I have learned to overcome.

I feel that I have been on both sides of the fence with my hearing loss, the solemn, quiet side that hides and is filled with self-blame, and also that side that takes a chance to soar at full potential. Believe me, the latter is much more joyful and rewarding, but it does take some work and persistence. A hearing loss is visual (people see it); therefore, discrimination and judgment are often passed. However, it is the approach that you choose to take and how you present yourself that will determine how you are regarded by others, respected by others, and called upon by others. It will make all of the difference in the world.

My experience has shown me that there will be times when we find ourselves facing stress and anxiety from simply handling the challenges from one day to the next. Let's face it, life can be difficult with a hearing loss. We struggle to stay afloat for an ordinary day, while in the midst, adjusting hearing aids, straining to hear, and frantically lip reading. We find that a day that started so simple becomes quite overwhelming. We listen, struggle to hear, and repeat this behavior and pattern again and again.

There is eventually a pileup of exhaustion that comes, and when you feel it is sometimes too much to bear, it's time to take a different route, understand that your way has not served you well, and that perhaps it's time to try a few take-charge strategies. The take-charge strategies that you will learn in this book will be enlightening, simply because I can relate to your struggle.

My tips are yours to use as well. They have enabled me to rise up in my difficult times; to avoid overthinking, to live in the present and prepare my mind to receive all that I have to offer; to always be at my best; to graduate at the top of many academic classes, excel in leadership positions, conquer great self-care habits, and mother a child, to name just a few of the miraculous happenings of my life. I am going to lay it all out on the table, the good and the bad. We are going to connect, and you will begin to understand why certain habits need to be embedded in your life, just like a trademark signature on a very good product.

Know that you are capable...

In life, when we set a goal to do anything, our first thought should be to know that we are capable; to simply know that we can get this done. This confidence only happens when you know your limits and abilities. When we know our limits, we will ask for help willingly, and with the right attitude, we will receive it. There will be some skills that you master in life and some that you simply suck at, but you have to understand that this is the case with every human being on this earth, not only you.

Let's take the analogy of bowling skills, for example. A bowling team has much more expertise in bowling than a few friends that simply gather spuriously a few times a year to "test out their skills" (as if they truly have any when they only bowl a few times a year). However, the bowling team has made it a mission to be the best at bowling, intending to be rewarded for their hard work. They study what other leagues are doing, subscribe to bowling media channels, and continuously research new strategies used by the league's biggest names. They are positioning themselves for excellence through knowledge while also empowering themselves and their team through knowledge. Knowledge is a powerful thing.

This book will help you understand how to cope so that you will have more peaceful days. It will help you begin to take the steps and determine the lifestyle that you want to make for yourself, so that you will reach your peak, even while facing a hearing loss. I have always believed that there are two ways to learn: Through books or experience. Myself, I don't prefer the latter. Let's take, for example, learning how disheartening it is to work in a discriminatory workplace (after all, they do exist). But truthfully, why go through that discriminatory workplace when you can simply read and learn how to avoid toxic work environments, or how to build your work environment to be non-discriminatory? It's your life, and it is totally your choice.

I want you to see my struggle and understand how I learned to advance past it; I have split my life into stages. I know that I had to live through some stages to be comfortable in the next. I know that this will pull you closer to me as a reader—to enable you to grow and gain compassion, to understand the story of one with a life that is similar to yours, or similar to a client, friend, or loved one that you wish to understand more.

That audiology visit described earlier was five years ago. I can honestly say that it was a dreadful day in my life because all I could feel was the worry of my life spinning out of control, and the fear of an even harder life ahead. I was suffering in sadness, unheard. I have grown accustomed to getting evaluations, for well over three decades now, to be precise. I've been getting these tests since I was four years old. I knew the routine, "raise your hand when you hear the beep" or "repeat the word that you hear me say."

Those were the famous words that the audiologist said to me, as she continued moving her equipment up and down to different levels, testing out my hearing. But this time, I had conveyed very few words, and I heard very few beeps. I held back tears, my spirit stumbled and crashed, barely hearing the words that she asked me to repeat. It was gut-wrenching and heartbreaking. My past hearing level was something that I had held onto with all of my might. I thrived on it with a passion, and never wanted to hear that it had declined, yet again.

My doctor came in; she talked to me, asking me if I had had any major surgeries on my ears, because my test seemed to show a substantial drop in my hearing level. "Nope," I told her. "And this is how you hear every day?" she asked. "Yes," I answered. With that answer, she said that she would be sure to write a wonderful letter of recommendation for a great cochlear implant program. I was a mother to a child. I was a good friend to others, listening in their times of need. I was a leader, a business owner, and a community resource to so many people. I had established myself and my life as an upbeat leader among people. How was I supposed to sustain my internal will to continue to perform as the leader, when I could barely hear what they were saying? Was all that I had been hearing emotionally driven through enthusiasm, but not physically possible? Oh, I was confused and frantic to say, the least.

She finished the hearing test and gave me a copy of my report. She told me that she would be in contact with me and that I would be receiving the full evaluation along with the letter of recommendation. I walked out of the office and to my car. I could barely hold back the tears. I climbed into my car, pulling the door shut. With tears streaming down my face, I sat and simply cried in complete stillness. I could not move. I felt utterly defeated. For many years, I had been telling myself that I was just fine, but this test said otherwise. At this time, I had not yet realized that inner power is much greater than external environments. I was waiting for the awakening that would help me find my true internal power, which would help me overcome this hearing loss. It was coming.

As a child, my eyes were my safe haven...

At the age of twelve years old, I began watching a family sitcom that came on tv once a week called *The Wonder Years*, which was a sitcom based on the character of Kevin Arnold. Kevin Arnold was a growing adolescent within a suburban middle-class family. Kevin (as an adult) narrated the storyline as he reflected on his childhood. It was a television show that I favored because it seemed to take viewers into the character's subconscious mind, or I will say, he shared his thoughts aloud, being hilarious to me. In other words, Kevin did a lot of self-questioning and a lot of self-assurance, as well. This show set the tone for self-questioning and years of wondering at this time in my life.

It came at the perfect time. My parents had just relocated to a nicer area of Washington, D.C., where my father had purchased a huge detached house. We moved in and fixed it up by gutting out everything, scraping wallpaper, and repainting. My family life was awesome. My mom was a teacher in the local school system, and my Dad was an electrician for the leading electricity service provider in the area, PEPCO (Potomac Electric Power Company). I grew up in the company of three sisters, Donna, Dominese, and Quintina. What I loved most about my childhood was our house, and the attic situated over the garage. It could only be entered through the master bedroom, which was my parents' room. Most children appreciate attics, but this attic was different. As I said earlier, we gutted out and cleaned the entire house of all that the former owner had left behind; however, we decided to leave cleaning out the attic for later. The previous owner had so much stuff in this attic, good stuff.

There were teddy bears, dolls, yarn and thread, pillows, and best of all, books. Yes, loads and loads of books. As we entered into the attic, along both sides, were huge closets of bookshelves. It soon became my very own secret hideout. I didn't jump at the chance to get the television remote; but I preferred to sneak to the attic to get a book. There were autobiographies, fiction, science fiction, history, cookbooks, and even atlas' and maps.

Reading became an escape for me. It didn't require me to be aware of my surroundings as much as listening and hearing did. I mean, you could have literally run a parade through my front door, and I would not have budged. Not because I was avoiding it, but simply because I was unaware. Reading allowed me to envision characters in stories; it was a world where I never missed a word because I was not listening, only reading.

My most memorable book was *Charlotte's Web* by E.B. White. I loved its colorful cover page and the story setting of a young girl who lived on a farm. I challenged myself to read this at eight-years-old because I wanted my reading to be fun. I also wanted to breed a new reading environment for myself. But most of all, I wanted to envision and follow the full story without worrying about volume or hearing, and this attic allowed me to do just that. Reading helped me expand my mind, rest my ears, calm my heart, and secure my confidence. So, I guess you could say I was a bit withdrawn, but I like to think that I was withdrawn in a good way—in a way that was beneficial to me.

I recently read an NIH (National Institutes of Health) article entitled "Self-Esteem in Hearing-Impaired Children: The Influence of Communication, Education, and Audiological Characteristics".[1] In this article, they presented that "sufficient self-esteem is extremely important for psychosocial functioning. It is hypothesized that hearing-impaired (HI) children have lower levels of self-esteem, because, among other things, they frequently experience lower language and communication skills." When I read this article, I began to think about how a child with lesser hearing might preserve her self-esteem by engrossing herself in more independent reading, so that is what I did! Kudos!

As I know it, my hearing loss is hereditary and has run throughout the family for well over three generations now. My grandfather, my father, uncle, and a few cousins were hearing disabled, and so was my beautiful twin sister and best friend. That's right! There's two of me! Awesome, right? Just kidding. She and I are not identical in our appearance, but she fought the battle of being hearing disabled as well, right alongside me.

She always deemed herself a protector over me (although I never asked her to do that) since her hearing disability was a little less severe. I think she just realized, during our childhood, how important it would be for me to have someone to lean on. She was very sweet throughout my childhood; she cared and was not afraid to show it. Although she had a hearing loss, too, as I said before, it was always diagnosed much less severe than mine. I knew this because Mrs. Tabinka, our audiologist, was very friendly, kind, and explanatory to my sister and me during our visits.

I didn't mind audiology visits in my younger years, but they weren't so exciting as time passed. Mrs. Tabinka always lined her office with toys, which were very inviting for a child, and she was extra friendly; but as I grew older, the toys didn't matter as much, as I began to pay attention more to why I was there, and what was going on with my hearing. She allowed me to ask questions and continually adjusted the headphones to make me comfortable while testing. I think just having my sister there to always hear, "Oh, yeah… Dominique's hearing is a little worse, but she will be fine," was quite bothersome as a child. However, as I reflect, I realize that she was about as kind as an audiologist could have been and that her words always had me leaving appointments feeling assured and safe.

My family contributed so much toward my comfort and adjustment. They repeated things across the dinner table, hollered up to the next level of the house, and made sure that I always felt included. Never once did I ever receive an insult from a family member. In fact, I've got a special tidbit of memory of how each of them helped me along my journey, which I will share in just a bit. My father, who suffered from a hearing loss as well, reminded me with my schoolwork that I was not intellectually challenged, but hearing challenged, meaning that I would be just fine. He never allowed me to take the loss personally or to become overwhelmed by it. He reminded me that I deserved just as much chance as the next person, if not more.

According to a recent WebMD article entitled *Help for Parents of Children with Hearing Loss*,[2] "Most children with hearing loss are born to parents with normal hearing. That means the entire family may have to learn about living with the condition." With this in mind, I can understand, as well, that each home is different and that some parents may not have been as familiar with it as my parents were.

However, my mom was not raised around the lesser hearing, so when it came about in her children, she decided to educate herself about it. Her sacrifices still astonish me to this day. Upon my placement in a regular education class at kindergarten, I received a teacher who insisted that I needed special education classes. My mom withdrew me, enrolling me into another school that was a few blocks away that accepted me into a regular education class. She then enrolled herself into a university to learn Special Education and soon became a Special Education teacher. She insisted that a hearing disability did not require the same level of special assistance that was often sought for learning disabilities (which she now taught). She inferred that by compiling regular education, a few accommodations, and my audiologist's recommendations, we would do just fine.

The field was full of opportunity, but she later relayed that taking the job as a special education teacher was her way of staying current with the special education laws in public schools. I love her for that. As the years progressed, she worked closely with my teachers. Many teachers chose front row seats in the class, or a chair beside their desk to accommodate me. They did a lot of reassuring and making eye contact with me for understanding, as my mom had asked them to. She made classroom management a lot easier for my teachers, which was helpful for them.

I can't say that she wasn't on to something (my mom, I mean) because I needed my teachers to understand my needs and make the necessary accommodations. Before the first grade—when I was diagnosed—I didn't pay much attention because I was still adjusting to hearing aids and learning classroom discipline. When I received them, the world and my surroundings made more sense, but it was still an adjustment. I loved my hearing aids; I never took them off. People stared often, but I didn't care. Child please, I could hear, and I wasn't giving that up for anybody. I mean, why would I? Why take your hearing aids out just to appease others, while leaving you in the dark? That never struck me as the thing to do at all. Everyone around me was going to have to adjust and accommodate, because I was going to hear like everyone else, and this hearing aid would allow me to do just that.

My adjustment to listening and following directions in class came slowly but surely because, in the previous years, I had not followed the flow of the class, due to my inability to hear without the hearing aids. Sometimes I didn't hear much, but that didn't stop me from talking and socializing. Go figure on that one... I was a motormouth. My first-grade teacher, Ms. Jones, was very nice, though. One day, she decided to make the class turkey soup for Thanksgiving, cutting up vegetables in front of us. Silly me stopped paying attention and got my head stuck in a chair. I cried so much that they ran to get my twin sister to calm me down, while the janitor unscrewed the chair. It was a hilarious day; it showed how venturesome I was as a child. I talked all night long at bedtime, making my father impatient. When I was younger, I had no idea that my hearing loss made me speak louder; because of this, he always caught me.

My sisters had a few tricks up their sleeves for me, too. They teased me as I sang the wrong lyrics to songs. They even played a game of sending me to my father when he beckoned, saying, "Daddy called you," when they had been called on themselves. My father grew frustrated at them and sad for me. One day, he had had enough and told me, "From now on, when I call somebody in the house, don't you come!" My sisters were mad, the cat was out of the bag, and all of the house errands and chores were now their responsibilities, as I sat around freely. I still laugh to this day at this story.

My sisters made my childhood beautiful. Whenever we went places, they made sure I was okay. My twin sister pretty much saved my life a few times, later in our high school years when we attended parties in rough areas of Washington, D.C. That didn't last long for me, though. Pretty soon, I learned to stop putting my life in danger by attending parties where I could not hear. I didn't favor those parties anyway. I was talkative, but I wasn't a party animal. I would have preferred to be at home reading a book and talking my parent's heads off about it. My family truly helped me to build my first great inner circle in my life, which showed me how vital relationships were in the early life of a child. When you've experienced loving relationships, then you know loving relationships.

By junior high school, I caught the bus to and from school, in congested traffic jams all year long. The city was very chaotic. When I speak of chaos, I mean low volume chaos. Sounds creepy, right? Yes, well, it was! "The severity of hearing impairment is categorized by how much louder volumes need to be set before they can detect a sound." Sounds were all around me, but I could only hear sounds at a certain decibel, like loud dump truck engines. Truck engines were always loud and boisterous. This is what I would describe as the most memorable sound in my childhood. Actions were everywhere (with minimal sounds) because there were so many people.

For the hearing disabled person, this means no ability to decipher some actions from others. Ambulances, kids playing, people running for buses, teenagers playing loud music, couples on dates, and the list goes on.

This can be quite overwhelming. While some can eavesdrop on conversations, that was never a possibility for me. Not that eavesdropping is a good thing, but on the crowded city streets of Washington, D.C., street smarts and discernment are requirements. Let me tell you how with an example: Imagine sitting on a crowded bus with other people who are in groups of two or more; some are even standing in aisles, talking, or laughing. Now, imagine that all conversations are low and difficult to interpret, and nothing is understood, or even pronounced to your understanding. How many times have you encountered this? And if you're not suffering from a hearing loss, how would you feel able only to watch your favorite sitcom or movie at minimal volume? Well, I bet you would start to regress sooner or later and seek ways to entertain yourself without your ears. Well, that was my world every day, before and after school. In the city growing up, it was very vibrant and tense, yet quiet.

I have learned that being able to decipher what's going on around can help you prepare for what's to come quite well. Here's another example: Let's say that you're sitting on the bus and you see a woman and man sitting beside each other, talking. She looks bothered, but you cannot make out what they're talking about. Hmmm… she gets off at the next stop, and he continues riding, but your stop is five minutes more.

He moves on to bothering someone else who welcomes him, but is later annoyed. She gets off at the next stop. Then, the following stop is yours. You get off, and so does he. Oh boy! He approaches you, trying to sell some stolen body wash in a grocery store bag. Well, your ears could have saved you from a rude encounter, if you had known what the two earlier conflicts were about. You could have easily walked away quickly, saying something like, "No thanks, Sir. I just went grocery shopping yesterday." Sound familiar?

Oh, yeah, I was pulled into situations like this very often; and because of these encounters throughout my childhood, I developed the desire to turn the volume down and regress from crowds and friends. In my heart, this would enable me to focus on preferred conversations and never miss a beat. But, of course, life doesn't work that way. This created impatience and sadness. I mean, really… who can regulate their ears?

There were also occasions that I missed what I wanted to hear so badly. Sometimes jokes are told, and you just weren't looking at the person who told the joke; the group laughs, you miss it, and regress once again. We will talk more about social skills later. Sometimes, this struggle will cause you to naturally develop the desire to regress backward out of the conversation, no matter how meaningful. The point is that dealing with a loss, as such, can work against you.

As I mentioned earlier, I was in what I call the "wonder years" of my life, trying to figure it all out subconsciously. Then, one day, while reading an assortment of books that I found in the attic, I read about body language; to understand body language was to become a great benefit to me later, but it was all just words for now. Why? Well, because I was regressing from all conversations and declining talking in groups. My two sisters were both cheerleaders, but I refused to try out for the team because I was afraid that I wouldn't hear the coach, Mrs. Turner, in the large gymnasium. I mean, why would I try to be a cheerleader? I missed so much already around our house. My mom repeatedly on edge, shouted up the stairs for me to do the dishes, and my sisters always had to tap me and say, "Mommy's calling you." It was embarrassing and frustrating every time.

My family meant well, they were patient and would speak loudly for me, but I just felt useless. I just couldn't expect everyone else, outside of my family, to do that for me.

I was beginning to favor one-on-one conversations. One friend, in particular, was very kind about this. Carla Cunningham was her name, and she had a great spirit. She was smart, as well. My ability to keep up with her in our studies helped me see that I was equally smart. Well, Carla's grace spoiled me for a while with one-on-one conversations. Carla and her sister, Rachel, also rode the bus home with my sisters and me. We were all best friends. We even started our Junior High School year with the same bookbags made by the "United Colors of Benetton"!

Then, one day Carla asked me to join the Pom Pom squad with her. I was hesitant, but I knew that I wanted to start to be a part of something. She explained that tryouts were easy and that we would have fun. I was comfortable with the coach, Mrs. Jennings, and decided to try out. I remember our practices in Mrs. Jennings' room as we made up routines to *Bell Biv DeVoe*, *Kid and Play*, and other great hip hop music artists. It was awesome! We blasted the music loudly as we rehearsed, and I started to follow the body language of others, that I had read about, while learning the dances. This was the beginning of an entirely new era of my life.

Once I made the tryouts, everyone just helped each other - that was teamwork. They would rewind music and repeat steps, and I learned that perfect hearing didn't make you capable of everything, that everyone else had their flaws as well. I began to become genuinely interested in conversations, smiled more, and showed them that I appreciated their repeated steps, and I learned the importance of teamwork. I also learned that I could add happiness to a team of peers and that those who truly cared about me would repeat it. We had our performances, and I never missed a beat because I was well-versed, and my memory skills were superb.

As a teenager, I applied the big secret of body language...

After developing these skills, I started to think about whether one skill could help another. For instance, will a better memory require less hearing? Will rehearsing help me to know it well enough to focus on not having to hear as much? Oh, my brain was overwhelmed with thoughts, just like Kevin Arnold, if not more. My wonder years were blossoming, and so was I. I was now beginning to look for ways to combat the fight of being challenged by my hearing. I had touched on other gifts and talents, and I was not going to let them fall prey to this hearing loss.

As time passed, I realized that I also had excellent writing, mathematics, testing, and reading comprehension skills. I mean, well, I had read a lot of books. Maybe the "escapes" of reading to avoid listening (and not hearing) turned out to be worthwhile. I moved onto high school and took part in a Pre-Engineering study at Dunbar Senior High School. There, I became a Varsity cheerleader and gained the same enjoyable experience of teamwork, rehearsal, and memorizing routines. I had an awesome coach, Ms. Burroughs, who emphasized respect, once again comfortable and grateful for being part of a team! Oh, but high school varsity was so much more extreme and daring than the small junior high school Pom Pom squad; we cheered on the sidelines of the gym during varsity basketball season, on the sideline of the fields for football season, and competed in cheerleading competitions for the city. It was a challenge, but my friends assisted me, and I learned what true friendship and acceptance were.

My adolescent years were unraveling wonderfully before my eyes, because I had learned teamwork, how to build relationships, and conquered how to read body language. Where exactly did I begin to pick up on body language? Oh, it was everywhere, but I like to think it started when I was a Pom Pom girl because I was determined not to take criticism personally, and I paid attention to teammates' body language when they had to redirect me. I had learned to watch hand gestures, head movements, clenched jaws, frowns, and on and on, which allowed me to help other people who were helping me. I want to propose to you the gift of getting a firsthand understanding and considering body language. I promise you that what I have to share about body language in a later chapter, will be both enlightening and life changing.

In sports, people act it out for you when teaching you, and in the midst of this, you begin to read body language. By the time I was in high school, I could walk down the hall and tell who had an attitude, without the need to hear a conversation. My eyes were my shield. I began to lip read conversations from across the room, just as I had done in practice. It's as if my fight to combat this had shown me other ways to decipher what was being said and done around me. I had grabbed the hearing disability by the bull horns and was riding freely! I graduated at the top of my class and was selected to meet the current President of the United States, Bill Clinton, who I later learned suffered from the same hearing loss type as well. This arousal of confidence through accomplishments quieted down my mind's tendency to question myself, my capabilities, and my tendency to overthink others' reactions. I had made myself an asset to others. They saw my skill before they saw my loss. They made efforts to work with me because we had invested in relationships, and they accepted me for who I was. I will talk more about growing relationships, as well, in a later chapter. But for now, I will say that high school was a pivotal time in my life that confirmed, for me, that I was a one-in-a-million—hearing disabled and all!

As a young adult, I maximized on building great relationships...

As a young adult, I was fresh off the press after college. Super excited about life, but I hadn't fully connected with my Recreation Therapy major in college, but for the most part, I enjoyed the curriculum. I knew that I wanted a career with an active, enjoyable day. . .one full of zest! I was at the age of ambition. If I read about it and liked it, I tried it. This was my approach to life and buying my first home at twenty-one and landing a real estate career at the young age of twenty-two—hearing loss and all. My older sister, Donna, dropped a real estate book in my lap one evening, and of course (being a bookworm), I read it. I jumped into it full throttle and never looked back. Pre-licensing class to get my real estate license was done in a flash, and I closed my first few deals within four months!

Real estate was active, live, and visual! It was exciting. There was no cubicle to sit in, no time clock to punch into every day, or an office coffee station (thank God). Oh no, that kind of traditional office work setup made me extremely tired. You always have to be so quiet in the office. People talked so low in offices! In real estate, it was about venturing outside of your environments to generate new clients, networking events, lunch partners, setting appointments, showing houses, and driving around the city. I loved it!

At the time, I was a full-time high school teacher, as well. I loved this work environment, too, because high school students are exciting and extremely loud, if I might say. So, yes, I was a young female entrepreneur educator with swag!

I loved my life. My clients loved me, and my students loved me. I always encouraged them to find their passion and excel at that. I helped them to understand that we may not all be good at everything, but each of us is wonderful at something. They just had to find it. This continued for nearly ten years, living the life, single, no responsibilities, playing the music as loud as I wanted. I was having lively conversations and even extremely jubilant relationships with friends; it didn't faze me that I was running what I had left of my hearing into the ground! Of course, I encountered my minor setbacks, but nothing too major. I learned to stop and listen more closely with clients and students, and I learned the importance of building relationships.

Building relationships enable people to "break the shell" with you and trust your expertise. This is something that worked wonders in my life. Clients referred clients, and my students trusted me. I was flourishing, but I was hearing at a level that was a little toxic. Aside from this factor of toxic hearing, I want to emphasize that you must understand the power of relationships. It's not an asset that we can afford to pass up. I will put it like this… many clients referred me because they appreciated my expertise and what I had done for them. Some clients come to me with their minds already made up that they want to work with me, even though they know that I suffer from a hearing loss. However, it doesn't matter to them because my reputation had already won the agreement with them. We will talk more about this in a later chapter as well.

As a mom, I learned to read my child...

Life was all well and good throughout my twenties. At thirty years old, my daughter came into my life, and I began to listen to my motherly intuition for tending to her well-being. I think what was most concerning for me, as a mother, was my inability to hear her cry at night. I had little sleep up until my daughter was about nine months. She was a great child—never sick, very happy, and self-sufficient, but it bothered me that I could not hear her unless I was looking at her. So, I began to look at her all of the time. I mean, literally following her little self everywhere. It may seem drastic, but you know what I'm talking about. Your eyes are your vision, well... at least they had become mine.

So, this was the game-changer in my life that helped me to slow down and understand what was going on around me more; to take time and learn to put her needs first. It was finally a time where visual cues and lip-reading couldn't help me because she was not talking or articulating sounds; she was just making baby sounds that I could not hear. I can't say that I was the gloomiest person about this; like everything in my life, I got over it, and when she turned two years old, I was thrilled that I could start to hear and recognize her voice. It was the sweetest sound, like no other, that I had ever heard. It was unconditional and dependent. It was a voice that I knew I had to answer every single time. I finally heard her voice, and I could recognize it.

What a great joy that was. Voice recognition is so very trivial in our lives. It's a complete home run when we have become accustomed to a person's voice. You may have even noticed this before. Some people stay around you so much that you can start to articulate and understand what they are saying without hearing every pronounced letter in a sentence. That is recognizing the voice in others.

As a person, I learned my inner strengths...

The hearing test that I spoke of at the beginning of the chapter was a few years after I had my daughter, which means that, by reading this book, you're all caught up on my life, and you are hearing from me now in my present life. But I have to admit, many facts and experiences have been omitted so far. In this book, and with all that you will learn and witness, there will be better times to share them. Some were sad and disheartening. Some were happy and uplifting.

I like to think that, even if they are good or bad, I have climbed mountains. I have gotten through the valley, thus creating a stronger person on the other side. Workplace discrimination (which I will share later) occurred when I returned to the workforce after having my child, but it made me a more persistent and proactive worker. I must say, any employer is blessed to have me at the speed and enthusiasm level for which I work now.

There is also the hardship of raising a child while countering a hearing loss. This was much harder in the beginning, but my relationship with my daughter is built on love, and there is not another person in the world that I would rather share my struggle with and receive comfort from than her. Children aren't judgmental—Chrissy is not. Yes, not only does my daughter adjust her voice loudly so that I can hear her, but I have to sometimes calm her down, bring her back to reality, and remind her that I will try to hear her at normal room volume, too. She is growing and changing, and she wants to take care of that part of my life. I have to remind her that the television doesn't have to be that loud or that I can try to hear at the level that she listens to, just to avoid interrupting the flow while she is watching her favorite television show.

Life keeps going and going, but it's up to us to make the most out of it. That is why I want you to read this entire book. I want to teach you how to "ride the bull by the horns", even on bad days where hearing aids are in the shop. Ride it by the horns. Even when your favorite song is on and your headphones are at their limit in volume, yet you can't hear, ride the bull by the horns. When you wake in the middle of the night, unable to remember where you put your hearing aid, or just trying to get a glass of water, then again, ride the bulls by the horns. It also means stepping forward, being *heard*, and speaking up to make sure your needs are met. You know them, but other people don't know what you need, and you have to be secure enough to tell them.

My life is blessed and under control now because I took the time to pause, quiet down my life, and analyze it. If there is one thing a hearing disabled person needs, it is quiet. We stretch our ears to hear, and we stretch our vocal cords to speak (not always hearing ourselves). We stretch our nerves, worried if we have interrupted another person. We stretch our cardiac system when we panic because we didn't hear something. When you practice this, you have uncovered something marvelous that will get you over the hump of life. So, settle your nerves and blood pressure to help your ears and vocal cords relax and function at normal levels.

Just wait it out and get through this book; I promise you that your days will be calmer, and your health will be better. I am sharing these things with you because I have to always stay assured that I am not letting my hearing loss limit me; it has to be adjusted, it has to be calmed, and it has to be soothed—and I *want* to share this with you. My victory. My joy. Only we can do this for ourselves by recognizing that a hearing loss does need that level of attention.

When you provide yourself with this level of attention, then you are providing yourself self-care, able to do more for yourself and others. Gone are the days where you say, "Oh, I'm not dealing with that today," or "I give up, this is just too much," or "I don't feel like socializing right now in my life." Nope, my friend, procrastination, and refusing to socialize are quite the same as running from problems that will always come up again.

Now, if you're ready, let's proceed to Chapter 2 so that we can begin to talk about what you need to know when dealing with the elephant in the room!

CHAPTER 2

Get this Elephant out of the Room: Understand What Makes Every Conversation a Success!

> *"What is important is not what you hear said, it's what you observe."*
>
> —Michael Connelly, Author

Understanding the elephant in the room...

So, what's your first thought when you walk into a room? Do you analyze the room size or the room setup? Do you look at the distance between the stage and the first row? Or, perhaps you check out how the microphone is set up for a presenter? As I have thought long about how I would convey this next concept, I have finally decided to call it what it is - "the elephant in the room."

The saying, "the elephant in the room," was created years ago by an author, Ivan Krylov, on a visit to a museum. He had realized that he had failed to notice the elephant exhibit. The metaphor represents a concept of size; the elephant is symbolic of something large, which has enormous energy felt by others in a common area. When we use the statement "the elephant in the room," we are saying that the massive problem is, in fact, bringing bad energy. It might be an unsettled disagreement between two friends at a dinner table, or the school board's refusal to talk about the school's declining test score problems at a meeting.

We all know what happens when someone throws the famous "elephant in the room" gesture into a conversation. They say something like, "Hey guys, can we please get the elephant out of the room here?" Everyone flinches because they question whether the comment is posed toward something that they may be hiding. They may even gesture, as well, to see who else may be bringing the elephant in the room, or to be blunt - the problem. The concept is that someone refuses to address a huge problem that is obvious to others.

"Removing the elephant" takes place by upping our confidence, getting over mishaps, and assuring ourselves that we are worth being heard. Our hearing loss does sometimes invoke an elephant into the room, and to avoid being caught in these situations, we then must consider a few take charge strategies and accommodations.

We need to know how trivial kicking the elephant out of the room is for those of us who harbor a hearing loss. It is intense and imperative because it brings extreme pressure and discomfort. You need to know that these situations will test your confidence, so let's talk about how to ace this test with flying colors! First, let's review a few steps that you can take to help yourself stay out of this valley. I want you to prepare yourself and to stop allowing the elephant into the room!

The truth is that there are so many types of rooms and venue setups that we will visit in our lives. With this concept of "the elephant in the room," you're going to have to address them; you're right on time because I'm going to push you every step of the way to do what's right for you!

Abracadabra!

We've all been to those tiring weddings where we don't hear a thing! Or, to your sister's graduation where everyone (except you) laughed and connected with the commencement speaker's heartfelt message. Well, there are a few ways to help you change all of this, if you're ready! No, it's not going to "abracadabra" you and reverse your hearing loss, but it will help you think ahead for what you need, and as a result of this, you will be better able to manage and control your emotions!

Some events you attend will reflect bad sound waves, and those of us who have hearing loss are significantly impacted by acoustic quality. Good acoustics are reflected in a room that has good sound waves that are sent clearly. That's not rocket science, right? This simply means that some events you attend will reflect bad sound waves (which you probably have experienced, but never applied a name to it), which is never a good thing. In case you were not aware, hard surfaces, such as tiled floors and paneled walls, can cause background noises to be repeated a few times as an echo. It is sometimes confusing and can, at times, seem unpleasant for hearing aid users.

Rooms that have thick carpet and drapes are usually the more favored room types for hearing aid users. Why? It's as simple as hard and soft. Hard surfaces, such as gym floors and marble bathroom tiles, are the bounciest environments for sound; the sounds bounce off the wall so easily that it can get very confusing. I kid you not. As I stated earlier, I actually read body language as a cheerleader.

The high school gymnasium was "large and hard," so to speak. A fellow teammate would start a cheer, and I would have to visually turn to see the movements just to recognize the sound because the sound was always a slight two seconds ahead of me. Crazy, right? Well, I can say, at least my struggle with these dreadful areas stopped after high school.

Imagine yourself working in a gym with a hearing loss. I've often thought about situations like this. At the end of the day, it's not very cool. Remember, as well, that sound waves lose energy as they travel. As humans, we can only hear within a limited distance, and sounds tend to travel shorter distances on foggy or windy days. Ever heard a train or a fire truck from far away? Now, think about that same train or fire truck as it breezes past you. As the fire truck and train gets lost in the distance, so does it's sound. That's just common sense.

An article presented by the National Academic Press stated that "because hearing loss tends to disrupt interpersonal communication and to interfere with the perception of meaningful environmental sounds, some individuals experience significant levels of distress as a result of their hearing problems." What does this mean for you?

It means that simply observing the setup or condition of a room will help you avoid becoming the 'elephant in the room.' You will avoid those uncomfortable moments where people feel pressured to consider your needs. For example, as a realtor, I show a lot of homes. This means that my work environment is always changing as I hop from one home to the next. However, I have learned to avoid talking in a bathroom or basement with an echo. Sometimes a theater or garage may have an echo as well. The point is to pick up on these room differences and make the adjustment.

As a precaution, sometimes I wait to get to a fully furnished and carpeted room or area, a draped room, or a walk-in closet to hold conversations. The great thing about this is that most of the time, my clients will follow my lead. You can up your game and take control in the same ways when you make a habit of thinking about room setups and the effect that they will have on your hearing. Trust me… it's worth it.

This is why it's always great to understand acoustics and sound waves. Some people also consider incorporating a loop system, if a venue offers it. A loop system transmits an audio signal directly into a hearing aid via a magnetic field. The system will also decrease background noises.

The equipment transmits sound from one or more microphones directly to the hearing aid via a telecoil. The telecoil can be fitted into most hearing aids. The benefit of this experience for me, when I attend events, is that it doesn't matter how far away that I sit, it still blocks out competing background noises. There may not be many venues that offer the loop system, but I encourage you to make some calls. You would probably be surprised at how many do offer this amenity.

Now, I want to introduce you to a few ways to compete with the 'elephant in the room.' In life, everything that you want to conquer should be a competition. When there is no competition, there is no fire, no purpose. And in this case, your biggest competitor is this big huge 'elephant in the room.' If you adopt these strategies, then you will be sure to communicate with ease because you have prepared yourself, actually convincing yourself that the 'elephant in the room' is definitely not you! Read on…

#1) Sharpen your lip-reading skills

One sure way to compete with the big bad 'elephant in the room' is to sharpen your lip-reading skills. This was a pet peeve of mine when I was younger, and it annoyed the crap out of my family. But, I later came to appreciate that I had picked it up as a voluntary craft during my childhood. What lip-reading creates for us is another technique that will allow us to listen by watching the facial movements, speech patterns, gestures, and expressions. One sure way to sharpen lip-reading skills is to test yourself by muting the television. This works like a charm, especially on a show that's your all-time favorite.

A United Kingdom charity group called Hearing Link says that "some people think of lip reading as a set of skills, while others believe it is an art." Personally, I prefer to view it as a divine art because creative arts allow us to create and solve. This goes much further than merely accomplishing the skill of lip reading. It means that you understand its true beauty, and you want to use it to solve problems (like 'elephants in the room') and create high energy (like smiling and warm spirits).

Lip reading is instrumental in deciphering words. You may hear every word in a sentence, except for a few, and lip-reading may help you decipher the last few that you missed. Kudos! What I find to be absolutely astounding is the majority of people that are completely unaware that you're reading their lips; then, suddenly, so much information becomes public. My take on it is that anyone with hearing loss should be using this gift, on a quest to use their eyes as a backup way to their ears, any time that they're able to.

It can become very second nature, when you think about it, since your eyes are one of your senses. Or, maybe it's just in my nature to be nosy. I'm dying laughing here. I must say, I have had the luxury of lip-reading far more than I should have in my early years. Sometimes, as a child, I would even drift away from a meal while out with my family to observe others' conversations.

Of course, with lip reading, you cannot show others that you are so heavily invested in their conversations, or they will be outraged. However, the chance of this happening is very slim because people are not often aware of the superb skill of lip reading or those who practice it. They don't look for it or even expect it. It's almost as if they don't even suspect it. I think some do suspect it from time to time, yet still refuse to say anything. It is sometimes out of fear, I guess. But, that's just my opinion. You would be surprised at the number of people that will minimize themselves to avoid friction with others. This example supports the reason that I want to encourage you to lip read more, as it can be a peaceful, yet valuable, art to practice.

When you develop a habit of lip-reading, you will come to understand that certain consonants require a specific formation of the lips. Of course, we know that the letters "s" and "c" are the opposite. "S" requires the teeth to clench, while "C" requires you to drop the jaw open. Any child that has received speech services knows how letters are formed through the skill of practicing pronunciation with a language pathologist.

You don't need to familiarize yourself with vowels to understand what someone is saying when lip-reading. In my opinion, vowels are always muted with lip pronunciation, and with practice in basic words and consonants, you can easily get around them. If you decide to familiarize yourself with the practice, then you will come to see that lip reading is not as difficult as you would think. In fact, it's rather interesting and daring. It is not a skill that would require you to come out of your comfort zone much.

Let's try an example! Let's say you're sitting at the airport and your flight has been delayed. You are one of the first customers off the plane to the sitting area. You watch a young lady making her way over to customer service, but where you are seated is too far to hear the conversation. You see that she seems upset. You can predict what the discussion might be about, but assumptions are never good, so you decide to lip read the conversation for practice.

She shows the customer service representative her ticket and throws both of her hands in the air saying, "OMG, this is crazy!" Well, we know through experience the body gestures of OMG, correct? Sure, we do. And then, because she is so ecstatic and dramatic, her consonants are heavily pronounced as she says, "This is crazy!"

Let's breakdown what she is saying and how common it is, shall we? The word "this" is very common, and you will quickly adjust to guessing common words with practice. It's a given, as with most common words (and, of it, that, there, etc.), for that matter. You will see that the words "the" or "that" are very similar, but never cause confusion, if you can manage to pick up the other words in the sentence.

The word "is" is stated so quickly that it's almost as if it's invisible. But that's alright, because it's not as important as the last word, which is "crazy." This is not a common word, but it can be easy to decipher because it tends to come with one physical expression. The "cr" in crazy is easy to see, as she scrunches her lips forward, and the "z" can be easy to get, as she emphasizes it most. We can see that it's a two-syllable word, which means she is not saying "this is cruel" or "this is crap." So, there you have it! If you're not attuned to lip reading, then you have just completed your first lip reading trial run! Congratulations!

There is a note of caution with lip reading, however. The Hearing Link also states that "lip reading requires deep concentration, and you will need to give yourself frequent breaks, especially at first. When you get the chance, close your eyes and relax for a few." I can attest to the truth in this statement, but I will admit that I will use up all of my energy to continue to be a part of the entire conversation. Lip reading requires strength in focusing and concentrating. Most of us divide our time between social media, checking emails, chatting, and working on tasks (among a few other things). So, yes... sorry to say, you will need to learn to "tune out the noise" to get this down pat. It will sharpen over time, but first, you must do a couple of things to boost your focus and concentration core.

#2) Talk with your doctor about a vitamin to boost your focus and memory

I'm no medical saint with a Ph.D. hanging on the wall of my office, but I can co-sign off on the power of focus and memory booster vitamins. Mine works wonders. If you are not very receptive to vitamins and such, let me give you a few pointers to help get you to your nearest nutrition shop! My vitamin choice is Gingko Smart, which supports mental alertness. This works wonders when lip-reading because you are alert and aware when things are happening, or when they aren't. If I cannot hear everything, then I definitely need my awareness. What helps to support this mental awareness is the Ginseng extract used. For years, I used only ginseng extract, and then I made the switch to Gingko Smart because of its combined memory skills, as well. That's right. This vitamin helped me not only to tune in to conversations but also recall and remember them for prolonged amounts of time. Talk about a blessing.

No, I am not a pharmacist or medical advisor, but this vitamin has worked wonders for me by sharpening my cognitive functioning and supporting my ability to concentrate. But hey, that's just my experience, as I said earlier, consider talking with your doctor or herbalist about this as well. I'm sure you will get the same advice from them when you relay that you are sharpening your lip-reading skills and would like to be able to concentrate. You just can't beat it!

Immerse yourself into the power of books

This strategy will probably be my hands-down, favorite point that I make out of this entire book. Upping your reading time will drastically increase your focus and concentration. There were times when I didn't read as much, so I struggled with conversations (both hearing and lip-reading). On the flip side, there were also times when I was an avid reader, and communication was smooth sailing. This is not rocket science—either you're feeding your mind, or you aren't. So, tell me again, how do we expect to create miraculous wonders out of a mind that you don't feed?

Please, it's like asking a baby to dance for the family when he is crying for his bottle. It's all the same, and it's even more prevalent in our day and age. We live in a generation surrounded by technology, crowded schedules, hour-to-hour traffic, and congested fast food lines. Believe me when I say you need a keen mind to focus on mastering lip reading. "In our internet-crazed world, attention is drawn in a million different directions at once, as we multi-task through every day. When you read a book, all of your attention is focused on the story—the rest of the world just falls away, and then you can immerse yourself into every fine detail that you're absorbing."

I agree with this author, that while lip-reading, you want your concentration to be solid as if you are reading a book. Ever notice how reading a book relaxes you, then you are more at ease with what you receive? That's what it does for me. I could never wrap my head around short magazine articles because they just ended too quickly. I'm talking about reading a book that will require an extended amount of time, discipline, and commitment. It is the same discipline and commitment that will have you lip-reading like LeBron James on a basketball court. Whoosh! My advice would be to give it fifteen to twenty minutes per day when you begin. It's best to get this time during the morning hours; my train commute works wonders for me. Here, there is nothing else to do, so it's the perfect opportunity to learn to tune others out.

Upping your reading game also has many other perks, such as increasing tranquility and promoting inner peace, improving your memory, and expanding your vocabulary. All of these assets will empower you to better speak and present yourself in public or to others. Increasing your reading will also build your analyzing skills. This may go over your head, but it works like dynamite with understanding your likes and dislikes, which is covered in another chapter. The ability to analyze can be used in both social and professional settings.

As I began this chapter, I talked about analyzing the room, and that was in relation to every type of room. So, yes, to become an avid reader is to become an avid analyzer, and you just can't beat that either! Below I have created a list of reasons to become a reader and the many incredible benefits that spring forth when you read more.

10 Great Reasons to Read	How this helps your hearing disability!
Develops Critical Thinking Skills	Great way to improve observations and actions of others, which take the stress out of having to hear it all!
Builds Vocabulary	Gives people a chance to see past your disability and view you as an intellect!
Upgrades Writing Skills	Impresses difficult people by writing it down sometimes and showing them with your superb writing skills!
Improves Focus and Concentration	Taps into your senses that allow you to focus, concentrate and then watch your hearing ability increase!

Drives Motivation	Reading inspiring books about the lives of others with heavier plights can lessen our burden on life!
Makes You Empathetic to Others	As we expect it, we must be able to give it. Reading and empathizing opens you up to compassion for others!
Improves Your Skills	Sharpening up in your industry, or excelling at you craft, will place you among the best at competition time!
Build Better Sleep Habits	Winding down at night with a book helps to calm our nerves, which assists our ears!
Increase Ability to Socialize	Sharing your latest reads takes the focus off of you and onto a great story, presenting you as well-informed!
Learn at Your Own Pace	Cut the online lecture and learn when you have time and read at the rate that you choose, using only your eyes!

#3) Adopt the power of meditating

In his book, entitled *Success Through Stillness*, Russel Simmons says that "When you learn to meditate, you will learn how to let your thoughts exist on their own, without getting too involved in them." (5) Take a minute and think about that. How many thoughts run through your head in a minute? How many in an hour? Better yet, a day? Much more than you would think, I promise you. My own testimony to meditation is that I practice it every day (before sleeping and at rising). I want to sleep well at night, and I want to perform well during the day. Ever since I have been persistent about meditating, surprisingly, I have been able to be much more productive, while at the same time living a more relaxed life.

The country where I live (America) is currently in the middle of this fad, saying, "I must look busy to show that I am successful." Quite frankly, it comes off as a little delusional to me. I cannot spend too much time with people who cannot slow down throughout their day. Seriously, if you are not taking time to enjoy meals, or if you feel life has too many decisions and nothing is productive, then maybe it's time to consider meditating.

Meditation has helped me to free up my mental space and to manage it well… cool, calm, and collectively. By managing my mental space better, I am able to calm my nerves and avoid becoming anxious. When we avoid anxiety, we tend to make better decisions because nothing is rushed. If you are multitasking on your job and trying to plan out the weekend simultaneously, that can become overwhelming. For example, not having enough time to pick out flight seats that best suit you, all because you didn't clear your head before taking on your next big tasks. And while we are on the issue of flights, please be sure to always alert attendants that you are hearing impaired. It makes the trip much safer.

Meditation is not as widely accepted as yoga, simply because meditation is individual, and yoga is often done in groups. But I do have to pitch this to you—there is a major difference. Most of our thoughts are repetitive, and when we stop them, we cut down on a room full of chaos in our minds. For instance, in the morning, as soon as I rise out of bed, my brain literally switches on. In accepting a new day mentally, I immediately (within five seconds) recall the happenings of yesterday. It's very frustrating, especially if yesterday didn't go well. So, instead of moving around to get ready, I brush my teeth, wash my face, drink a full glass of water and sit right back down in my meditation space. I set the timer on my phone to twenty minutes (without glancing at my text messages or emails), and I push the go button as the clock counts down. I meditate for a full twenty minutes every day, and at night, I repeat the same process before bed.

Ironically, the truth is that, after taking on this wonderful habit, I would not go a day now without it. Why get started in chaos when you can ease your way into the day… When you can flow with your day and organize your thoughts and prioritize? That's what meditation does in the morning. It gives us a chance to touch on our inner self-guidance, and, in that way, we can take care of ourselves before we enter the world, giving our lives over to every need that we have to fulfill. Staring into the darkness and listening to my breathing has even helped me reach my inner being to maximize my hearing. After meditating for a prolonged time (beyond a few months), I began to use my hearing more because I relaxed more. I was less anxious internally, regardless of what I was doing. Whether I was communicating with others, listening, working, or caring for others, it created a joy within me that I definitely cannot and will not live without.

#4) Monitor room setups for good vision and adequate lighting

Something else that I want to be clear about is the need for good vision and adequate lighting in your environment when you are practicing lip reading. It's pretty much common sense if you ask me. There are not many lips or facial expressions that you can read in a dark restaurant, or with the sun shining down on you at an outdoor wedding. In these cases, you will have to be confident enough to bring it to others' attention and have them adjust the environment (maybe move to an area of better lighting or away from extremely sunny areas) to suit your need. When people stand with their backs to a window, you may even have to politely gesture them to another location.

I will be the first to say that, in my many years of nudging folks and speaking up for what I need, I have learned that many people don't mind this at all. So, if you have never spoken up for what you need because the sun is blocking you or there's poor lighting, then I say give it a try! You will love yourself for it! Just remember to anticipate positive outcomes. As a lip reader, when I focus on one legible face and launch into a conversation, then something clicks. Right then, I feel something extraordinary... *human connection!*

If you need a single valid reason to lip read, then I would say (with vibrancy), do it for friends and family who love you! It will provide them with a less stressful experience, and you will be received as more empathetic with loved ones. Family and friends can be very genuine with us, but sometimes in stressful and challenging times, they can't find the patience to listen. However, if you come equipped with the lip-reading skills (trading one sense for another), they would respect you more. This may even spring forth a desire within them to adjust their actions for you, as well.

#5) Understand your level of hearing loss severity

Your hearing loss severity level does have a considerable effect on the ease with which you can pick up sounds at different levels of loudness or frequency. But let me stay out of the "audiology jargon" and simply say this: There are solutions to better your hearing, but you must be aware of your severity loss levels to understand what's useful for you and what's not.

When I had first graduated from college, I once mistakenly bought a hearing aid online that was geared towards mild hearing loss, while my hearing was categorized as severely hearing disabled. Ouch!

I waited eagerly for the FedEx package containing my new hearing aid to arrive for nearly a week. Once it arrived, I ripped open the package, and checkmate! I had done it! I was ecstatic and flabbergasted! I had substituted my $2,000 hearing aid for one that only cost $199. It had to be a miracle! I was astounded. I thought of all of the audiologists and wondered why they never recommended this brand. Well, it was too late now... to hell with them anyway!

I quickly assembled it (because for $200, it didn't have a fitted mold) and placed the battery in. Then, I placed it in my ear, and absolutely nothing happened. It looks like I got checkmated! Gypped. Jived. Whatever you want to call it, but those hearing aids produced no sound for me and were of no benefit to me whatsoever. I cried and cried and cried. If only I had read about the different levels of hearing severity. No wonder my original hearing aids were so costly, I thought.

Understanding the level of your hearing will provide you with confidence, and hopefully, a desire to familiarize yourself with what you can or cannot hear. Many sometimes feel reluctant to learn it, but we must remember, the quicker we accept, the faster everyone else will. Or how strongly we can convey our needs, the better others can suit our needs. I have always been familiar with what I was able to hear, but it wasn't until I reached young adulthood that I had to begin to speak of it more with those who cared about me.

I began to connect with people who genuinely wanted to see me excel. With this, always came the question, "So, what can you hear?" or "What volume is too low for me to talk at?" They all pursued this with good intent, but I often became stuck because, silly me, I had not taken the time to read and learn about it to prepare those around me. Here is a quick suggestion that will turn all of this worry into water under the bridge: Rather than measuring, comparing, and evaluating yourself, consider simply observing yourself and then accepting yourself.

In case you are not very familiar with hearing levels, here is a breakdown of the different levels of hearing, as it pertains to decibels. There are four levels of hearing loss, which can be measured by the ability someone can hear the quietest sounds.

There is **mild hearing loss,** which carries the minimal loss effect. This loss level means the person can hear between 25 and 40 dB. This means that the sound would have to measure between 25 and 40 dB in order for the mildly hearing disabled to hear it. Those mildly disabled are often annoyed by noisy rooms, but that's all; they may even be able to avoid needing to wear a hearing aid. Then there is **moderate hearing loss,** which requires a hearing aid, but not the most powerful aids are required. They hear the quietest sounds between 40 and 75 dB.

After moderate, the chart climbs to **severe hearing loss,** which is always in dire need of a powerful hearing aid, and usually develops lip-reading skills for assistance. The level of sound needed for this level is between 70 and 95 dB. Finally, we come to **profound hearing loss**. I call this group the brave runners! They venture forth without the use of sound and depend solely on lip-reading and sign language. Sounds must be made at 95 dB in order for this group to hear them. The brave runners live a life of luxury in sign language, as it's sometimes viewed as a language of awe and secret.

Level of Severity	Decibels	Hearing Aid Devices Used
Mild	25 to 40 dB	Not necessary
Moderate	40 to 75 dB	Optional, but recommended
Severe	70 to 95 dB	Highly recommended
Profoundly	95 dB+	Not recommended

How does identifying your level of hearing loss help you in life? Well, that's pretty simple. Knowing it allows you to speak on it, which will enable you to comfortably explain it to others. It also exemplifies confidence to others when you are able to speak of it with a good understanding. Over the years, I have learned the real power of this. Whether you're talking to employers, meeting neighbors at the park, or out on a date, you will invite the "elephant into the room," if you cannot confidently speak on your hearing loss with no shame and with ever-extending confidence. It's just that simple.

The funny thing about communication is that when we meet people (no matter what country of origin, or culture), they often emulate us; they stand the way we do, feel the way we do, and speak with the same energy we use. This is all a part of human connection, so as I have always said, "Place into the universe what you want and watch it come back to you ten-fold." If you place optimism, charm, and confidence, then you will receive optimism, charm, and confidence. Isn't that a beautiful thing, indeed! It's a given, and it's the way that the world works.

#6) Consider learning sign language

Sign language allows us to become better listeners. I learned this firsthand by taking sign language in college during my senior year. The instructor (who was a friend of mine) asked me to take her class and learn the IDEA (Individuals with Disabilities Education Act) LAW. Anyway, to make a long story short, it was an intimate and quiet classroom experience. No one was allowed to talk, but instead, they laughed a lot, filled with joy as they pushed themselves to communicate outside of their comfort zone. And that is precisely what sign language is: "A language learned outside of your comfort zone" because everything spoken had to be done by signing (which we are not used to). It was awesome, as well as a test for me, who had come to love talking.

If you consider enrolling in a course, I would say to ask a friend or family member to accompany you to learn it. This way, the "homework" will be easy. In sign language classes, what's most important is taking what you are learning and applying it in your life. Indeed, the English language is a lot in itself, so it would make sense to put it into practice as you learn so that it will not feel like a bunch of "untouched" information after the course.

Here's another thought: When learning American Sign Language, your ideas are physically formed (for instance, man is symbolized by two hands grabbing at the front of the face). There are many dynamics involved, which can be fun; you will begin to check your understanding consistently. This will make you a better listener. The communication of ideas is more precise and situation oriented. In other words, if you are discussing an upcoming birthday party, then you will be reviewing words that have "happy" gestures, such as "cake," "party hat," or "music." This makes sign language more interesting to the beginner as they laugh and learn more words. Those are valuable skills, which non-signers often do not develop. If you have a growing desire to learn sign language, your first stop should be either a community college or library for inexpensive classes. You may even want to consider a sign language dictionary with a partner, or a beginner's course.

Let me stop here and shed some light on one question: Which should I learn first, sign language or lip-reading? Since I have an adjusted hearing loss and not a total hearing loss, then I would choose the latter because when we learn to read lips, we can move among ordinary hearers, so this is very useful. Sign language skills are great to learn, but we must look at how we spend our time in terms of numbers and opportunities. There will not be many who know and understand sign language, but there will be easy ways to adjust to reading lips throughout many environments, if that makes sense. I have enormous respect for those who practice sign language; it should be pursued by all who are hard of hearing, but in my opinion, only after you have learned the skill of lip reading.

#7) Consider suggesting printed instructions for major events

Weddings, funerals, and graduations are extremely organized, so being out of place can be very costly to others. I always appreciate a printed, running order for wedding photoshoots, with instructions as to where I need to be and what time to be there. If you are asked to take part in a wedding or large event, consider asking the organizer to write out any crucial instructions that they may have for you ahead of time to minimize your needs on the big day. This will bring calmness and clarity to both the organizer and you on that big day.

In 2017, I graduated from graduate school, along with a commencement of nearly three thousand graduates. The arena was huge, and thankfully, most of our instructions were printed. Before I arrived at the arena, I was emailed instructions for which gate to enter, and which parking area was for graduates. The courses that I took were online, so I didn't know many people by name. Below the arena, in the undercroft area, everything was printed out for us, even area seating maps; we were directed to our seats and then led onto the stage to receive our degrees. It was awesome and stress-free.

But how do they address large audiences, and how do we hear in events like stadium-sized graduations? Oh dear, it can be appalling, and I, too, share the frustrations. Again, you need to prepare yourself emotionally, as well as physically. Technology has enabled us to connect Bluetooth devices to microphones; consider calling ahead to see if the microphone is compatible with your hearing device. If you miss this step, then I would encourage you to consider sitting as close to the stage as possible, even if you're not sitting with loved ones. There is nothing more disheartening than everyone sharing in the speaker's joy and pain, except you.

For me, these were the most trying times being hearing impaired. But again, remember the power of meditation and book reading, as I shared earlier. If you meditate often, your nerves will be relaxed enough to follow the speaker; if you're practicing daily reading, then your vocabulary will be sharper, and your mind won't have to work overtime. Just remember, with everything, preparation is key. Whether you choose to call ahead or meditate, you will be prepared, which will make the event more enjoyable.

#8) When out of town, ask for hotel rooms with vibrating/ flashing fire alarms

Are you looking to take a trip soon? Here's an idea: for overnight hotel trips, always make sure that your room contains flashing/vibrating fire alarms. Many hotels are now required to be deaf-friendly. This means that they must provide an evacuation plan for guests with disabilities. The alarms sound at 65 dB most of the time. This sound should be enough for most severely, mild, and moderate hearing loss people to hear. For those with profound hearing loss, a flashing or vibrating (or both) alarm is recommended. And boy, I've got a story for this one, too. I'm serious… it's amazing the experiences that we incur with a hearing loss, and I'm sure that you have your share, as well.

So, picture this… it's my first year of college, and I'm sleeping in my dormitory bed when the overseer for the dorms decides that she wants to perform a fire drill sporadically. Hmmph, silly me slept right through the fire drill. My twin sister, who was my roommate, came to the room ecstatically after standing outside for ten minutes with everyone else. "Did you actually sleep through a fire drill?" She was very bothered. I told you guys she was a worrier and protector of me. The others heard about it, and pretty soon, the Dean required a flashing alarm to be installed in my room immediately! It helped.

Luckily, we never encountered a real fire because I could never miss the flashing lights in my dorm room, even if I wanted to. Sometimes, our eyes save us. This, we know. It should be one of the major takeaways of this book, as well. "To that for which the ears do not hear, then the eyes are there."

You, of course, want to be sure to take advantage of public screened PA systems. I love the PA systems at the courthouse in my area. They are very specified. They give precise information, and continually even throw a map onto the screen for directions and room locations. Years ago, everyone who walked into the courthouse stood in a line, asking the same questions about what room they were supposed to go to. And while I'm thinking about the courthouse, let me say this: Never, never, never subject yourself to jury duty.

#9) Get a permanent letter of excusal from jury duty

I would say to get yourself a letter of excusal the next time that you visit the audiologist. It's gravely important. I'm not, by any chance, saying that we can't do it, but we shouldn't have to. Personally, I don't want to. All of my experiences in the courthouse have been terrible when it comes to my hearing.

Then you have to be so humble that it's difficult to ask for what you need. Now, imagine sitting among the other jurors, but you're the only one without the scoop. I can honestly say that I have no stories about being a juror, because I have never placed the pressure on myself. The reality is that I need to be accommodated, and, many times, the legal system is just not willing to do that. But I won't become biased, to each his own. I just don't recommend it.

#10) Make use of the buddy system when traveling

No matter how old I get, I'm never too old to use the buddy system. I've had the experience of cruising alone and with groups, and I have to say, the latter is preferred. Whether it's Cancun, Barbados, or Paris, it's all unfamiliar, and that brings a challenge to everybody. I'm a big fan of cruises! I love walking along the open decks by the water while the ship is at sea. I love dressing for dinner, and the great Broadway shows they offer. Mostly, I love that I can eat my heart out, although I have learned to take it easy over the years, or I will return home five pounds heavier.

For a few years, I tried group cruises with my sisters, then coworkers. Then people annoyed me because we always had to plan what the entire group wanted to do. Uggghhh! It was nerve-racking, and during a time in my life when I wanted what I wanted. You know what I'm talking about; sometimes, we are just more patient than others, but this was not one of those times. So, the next cruise I took was with my sisters. We had a great time, but I was still choosy about the excursions.

And then, I went on a cruise with a good friend. She and I enjoyed the first few days, but we clashed for the two remaining days. It was a headache. Finally, I decided to go and take a cruise by myself. "Forget it!" I told myself. "I don't need anyone to come with me." And boy, how wrong I was.

For the bulk of the cruise I ate alone; I attended shows alone. We docked in the Bahamas and Jamaica, which were both places I had cruised to before. The first pier in the Bahamas was nice and friendly because the shopping center was right along the pier. However, I shopped quickly and returned to the boat because I couldn't hear much of the rapport among the locals. When I saw how uncomfortable I was in the Bahamas, I didn't bother disembarking in Jamaica. I made the most of the big open pool on the Lido Deck while everyone else explored Jamaica. As we set sail to return home, I realized that I had made an awful mistake coming alone. More than anything, I had not had intimate conversations with anyone in nearly five days. I was tormented.

Don't get me wrong, the food and entertainment had been fantastic, but when you're around that number of people (nearly 2000), you're going to want to talk with others. Even though I wasn't able to choose all of the outings with my buddies in previous cruises, they relayed information, encouraged me, and comforted me. Getting along is trivial; one thing it takes first is getting over yourself. For my last cruise a year ago, I took my Mom and my daughter, and it was awesome! They had as much fun as I did.

Still, at times, even our favorite places could have a poor setup. This is one of my biggest struggles. Do I stay at home? Do I go out? Many times, we just don't get the favor of choosing the setup, but that doesn't mean that we have to stay home.

#11) Take a deep breath and adjust emotionally to mega buildings

My present church seats thousands of people. It is what many today call a Mega Church. I was a bit skeptical about joining at first, but I had to adjust and make myself comfortable there. This meant checking my confidence and controlling my emotions. I was a bit shy about not hearing the program when I first arrived. I would leave without getting the full message. Walking, saddened, to the parking lot had become a norm. And then I thought to myself, *what in the world? Why keep coming to church when you cannot hear?* Large audiences suck, and I know this because I have been the victim of being seated in the back of large audiences. But I have to say this was partially my fault.

After a while, I decided that enough was enough; I would stop leaving without hearing the message. These were places where I had control over where I sat, and yet, I still chose to sit in the back of this massive audience! "Come on, Dominique! You're doing this to yourself," I would remind myself. I didn't want to miss a lot, so I decided to speak up for myself instead. Any large room that allows you to choose your seat, don't be afraid to do that. Hint, hint, you're gonna need it. As the ushers welcomed me forward, I began to faithfully seat myself right behind the reserved section of deacons. This section was only about three or four rows back. It was excellent! I came, I joined in, I heard the message. After a while, nothing stopped me from plunging right for the front.

After a while, I realized something that was absolutely cool. I noticed that my pastor was reading from captioned slides. When he shared a message, he looked ahead to a screen that was hanging above the audience. So, I learned to sit at an angle where I could follow him with his slides and keep up. It has been remarkable. I have to admit that we don't get blessings like that a lot. No siree! We find videos on YouTube for the most important topics without captioning; there are still even a few shows and Netflix movies without captioning.

The point that I want to convey to you in this section, however, is never to fear large room sizes. What I mean by large room sizes are basketball gymnasiums, concert halls, theaters, megachurches, and so on! You have to prepare yourself for this because large events are more of a trend in our day and age. So, make an effort to figure out how you can adjust.

Try getting there twenty minutes before a performance starts, or as I mentioned earlier, look for the seating chart online, email, or call customer service for one. I promise you that it's worth it to go the extra mile to suit yourself. Remember, we use our eyes a lot, and without the ability to see, my friend, we feel we are doomed. It would be a struggle to sit behind a tall person, but maybe you can change that by arriving early.

In large room sizes, there is also more excitement with a larger number of people, so brace yourselves for the unheard. Yes, it's bound to happen—the tidbits here and there that you will not hear alongside so many others. It can work against my spirit a little bit, and then I remember why I am there and continue to make the most of it. Sometimes, there is also the use of low microphones or taking questions from the audience, which can be bothersome as well. It all can get a little frustrating, but as long as I can stay on point with what's happening, I will not get too fidgety.

I have acquired years of experience to know that it doesn't help to get into my feelings. This is why, most of the time, I will use a captioning device in movie theaters. Glory to the person who decided to place captioning devices in theaters. I will tell you that I was almost done frequenting movie theaters. I would actually wait for good movies to come on Netflix or cable tv. Now, these hearing devices make the experience much more pleasant, and the movie makes so much more sense when you can hear everything.

#12) Consider a hearing aid/Bluetooth device

Ever heard the phrase "save the best for last"? Well, that is exactly what I did in this chapter because I wanted you to leave with the knowledge of all of the previous items, but I want you to listen carefully to the capabilities of this last item. Times are changing, and technology is taking us much further. We have iPads and iPods, so communication has gone a whole lot further than phone lines. As for myself, I am a huge fan of Netflix, and I love my iPad, too. I begin my day with my iPad, use it throughout the day with my calendar, and check it at night to review the following day's task. But I think that I left out an awful lot. I converse on social media with it; I watch YouTube videos and Netflix shows on it all day, every day. I research for books with it and set appointments with it. I listen to audible books and podcasts with it, hold webinar classes with it, and attend online meetings from time to time. And in the midst of this, I never have to remove my hearing aids. What's the secret? I'm glad that you asked… hearing aid with Bluetooth compatibility.

This last strategy is the most pertinent because it is the one that is going to help you keep up with *the Joneses*. It's going to help you use technology to your advantage. What's the use of wearing a hearing aid if you have to take it off for every phone call? And let me remind you that you are not alone with that either, because there was a time in my life that I was doing just this. My point is clear and short. Invest in it, learn it. Just as the world was overtaken by cell phones, our community needs to embrace the hearing aid Bluetooth device. It's to die for.

#13) Embrace the small steps

Becoming a top-level, confident being while possessing a hearing loss doesn't just happen overnight. So, be sure to make a note of your small successes, or simply put, embrace the small steps. You may have finally spoken up at a staff meeting or decided to share an eight-line poem at open mic night. It's not always realistic for everyone to reach into the room, grab the "elephant," and carry him out of the room (as though that is even possible). I was recently watching the Braxton Sisters on Iyanla Vanzant's Show, "Fix My Life", which aired years ago. Tamar Braxton was having a fit (as always) and making herself appear to be the black sheep of the family. Better yet, she was bringing the "elephant into the room." Evelyn Braxton reached over to her child in a time of conflict (for Tamar) and told her, "there is a way to do it". Today, I say the same thing, *there is a way to do it.* Start small and congratulate yourself.

One sure way to put small steps into your life rotation is to keep a journal and score yourself. Do you have something that you want to accomplish? Consistency or perseverance? One of my biggest life challenges was accomplished when I placed it onto an index card. I decided that I would observe my days and start to monitor myself better. To save my life, I couldn't figure out why I could not be as consistent as I desired to be. Yet, I had heard that consistency was the beginning key to mastering wonderful things.

In this same way that I mastered consistency, maybe you could master perseverance to attend unfavorable events that just don't always have the setup. Just remember that you have to take the right mindset along with you, as well, in order for the event to serve its purpose and to be beneficial to you. Okay, so I will say it... lose the attitude and give it a try! Choose a few events over the course of the next three months. Write them down on an index card. Check off each event and place the that you attended. Briefly write down what was favorable and unfavorable about the event setup; rate yourself as one to ten on how satisfied you were at attending the event. This means your rate should be a combination of interaction, attitude, listening skills, cooperation, and overall enjoyment. At the end of ninety days, create a scoreboard for your system. The idea is to encourage a better attitude, so try to find out more about the events that you liked when you come back to your card.

Give yourself a score based on the overall number of events. For instance, if you attended twelve events (one per week), divide your total number of rated points for ninety days by twelve. You will love yourself for it. This will give you an A, B, C, D, or F score, and you will see where your problem is. Numbers and visuals do a lot for us. Sometimes when we see our progress on paper, we can truly give ourselves credit and move on to the bigger fish to fry!

Self-Love is the key...

I hope that this chapter has provided you with great resources, but most importantly, an abundance of understanding of the many tools available for you. However, when dealing with the "elephant in the room," the ultimate tool is self-love, which is manifested through self-acceptance, which we will discuss in the next chapter. Self-love is the key to building your ultimate life satisfaction as hearing impaired. Self-love will encourage you to buy the Bluetooth. Self-love will motivate you to try lip reading. Self-love will help you to develop the esteem to deal with adversity.

There is no one tool for countering every issue we come upon, but sometimes, by continually strengthening your self-love, you will be provided a path to more effortless conversations. And there you have it—the "elephant" is out of the room!

CHAPTER 3

You Can't Soar While Hiding Among the Bushes... Know that It All Starts with Your Own Acceptance of Self!

> *"Peace comes from within. Do not seek it without."*
> —Siddhārtha Gautama

Dare to partake of the dazzling hearing device...

In my opinion, glasses have become globally accepted as a modern trend — they are great conversation starters and make a statement when they bling across the faces of millions of people worldwide. It's as if the visually impaired community said, "This is me, accept it or not, I don't care, deal with it."

However, there is still much progress to be made when it comes to the acceptance of hearing devices, which are often hidden among the lesser hearing society. The way hearing devices are currently presented in today's world doesn't do them equal justice, especially considering the essential service they provide.

In this chapter, I want to encourage you to refuse to hide a hearing aid and stand proud while wearing it. I want you to know that a hearing aid will be accepted when you accept it, it's as simple as that. This will allow you to truly be yourself, which is why I want to help you understand what self-acceptance is and why it is something we need to embrace.

Especially when you consider that you've got this hunk of a hearing aid sitting in your ear for the entire world to see, acceptance of yourself is crucial. But, let's envision for a moment, a world that accepts hearing aids just as it does headphones when worn at a silent disco party, or a beautiful prom queen praised for her electrifying hearing aid jewelry that matches her dress, or a well-suited man with gold-plated hearing aid Bluetooth device stepping out of his Ferrari.

Like everything in life, it's how you present it. Is it a piece of junk or a dazzling accessory? Is it a hindrance or a conversation starter? Yes, I bet that's a positive perspective you never quite thought of when thinking of hearing aid devices, but it's sad to say, it is where many of us are. I remember a few years ago when my hairstylist convinced me to get a nice pair of eccentric glasses to business network more and build conversations. It was the new fad, according to her. I connected with the vendor on Instagram and ordered a pair, but I barely wore them; they were just too big, red, and bloomy. I didn't last very long with the trendy glasses, but the next time I visited my audiologist, I asked for a beautiful dazzling plum-colored ear mold, and well, the rest is history. My most recently purchased hearing device is a combination of hot pink and champagne.

Nope, I am not asking you to wear a pair of oversized glasses, but maybe challenge yourself a bit with a beautiful hearing aid? A significant takeaway with the hearing aid is that, unlike the glasses, the size doesn't have to change, only the colors.

Why are most hearing aid colors earth-toned colored, such as brown, tan, or dove, anyway? To blend better into different skin complexions is the answer. It's as if doctors in the earlier days said, "Okay, with that color, they shouldn't be able to pick up on it"… uggghhh. Exactly my point—the way of the past has been to hide the hearing aid and look how far it has gotten us. Not very far. Indeed, it makes no sense to hide something so beneficial to your existence just to avoid the dislikes of others. I want to encourage you to learn and to practice both self-acceptance and hearing aid acceptance. Remember this, "having a hearing aid that is colorful and sleek is analogous, in many ways, to having the latest smartphone in a hip, new color." Wow, that's food for thought!

Now, about self-acceptance. Without a strong, positive foundation built on self-acceptance and self-love, you run the risk of rejecting hearing devices; this will only cause you to suffer in silence. So, what's the deal with this self-love, self-acceptance pitch, anyway? Well, if you've never stopped to fully understand it, let me just say, self-love rocks! It's powerful, by golly, it's exuberant, and it's completely underrated! No one is going to love you like yourself. There is no better person to learn to love than yourself. Self-love makes you more aware of your own needs so that you can convey them to others. Jackpot!

Also, there is a certain level of acceptance that we must achieve to wear something so visual as a hearing aid! Life has its ups and downs; we must push forward in our decision by refusing to hide a hearing aid in hard times, as we did when we walked confidently into a room where we would be outright accepted.

By increasing your self-love, you will decrease the desire to hide the hearing aid and appease others. We cannot, and should not, allow the views and inability of others who cannot accept it to make us feel like we cannot accept it. Yes, we do come upon those who are hesitant and reluctant to work with us or cooperate with us, which is a shame. But tell me, when did the ignorant get to decide your fate? This is the moment to put your blossoming hearing aid on, hit play on your Bluetooth, pull out your sunglasses, and glide across the room in sheer fame, loving the way that you are wonderfully made!

What's meant for you is for you; it's as simple as that

Life presents its challenges, but remember, what's meant for us is meant for us. It's just that simple. What is not simple is questioning whether you should be a part of something because others cannot adjust their feelings to accept you. Your decision to join events, clubs, ministries, meetings, is always your decision. Stop and ask yourself, "How do I feel about participating?" If it is something that you want to participate in, then you must muster up some self-love and get rid of any crazy illusion that you don't belong, or that your hearing aid will be a problem in this. It is a part of who you are, and when push comes to shove, more than likely, this hearing aid does tons more for you than any person standing among you.

The worst feeling is to not be comfortable with yourself.

Hiding the hearing aid can arise as a desire in us because of where society is presently in its non-acceptance of others, it's judgmental ways, and simply, the insults faced when we are just merely trying to survive or participate. Embracing self-love will allow you to see that self-acceptance must come first, and then everything else will fall in line. People will accept you. You will make more friends. Groups will marvel at your participation and the gifts that you share, but this first means conquering self-acceptance.

It is my personal belief that in our present-day and time, people have turned their backs on, not only the disabled population, but the elderly population, the young adult population, and many other populations. I want this to be a strong self-motivating area in your life, simply because of this lack of empathy towards our population. Society has decreased its accountability; therefore, in turn, we must push forth and strive to always be at our best.

When we decide that we want to be at our best and perform well, we do not permit society to determine what we are capable of, or our potential for success; we are not allowing the realities of today to be the basis for which we set our lives and relationships. Does it matter that every YouTube video is not captioned? Does it matter that some movie theaters still have not invested in captioning devices? Should this diminish our happiness when we see that society, in some ways, has failed us? Well, I think you know my answer to that. Not at all!

"The Department of Justice (DOJ) recently issued regulations requiring digital movie theaters to operate and maintain the equipment necessary to provide closed captioning and audio descriptions at the movie patron's seat, whenever showing a digital movie... however, the final rule does not obligate movie theaters to provide captioning if the movie is not already available with captioning."

I shared that research finding with you to provide a realistic example. I wanted to remind you that everyone isn't going to conform to make your life comfortable. Guess what? It's not their job. It's yours. This statement about movie theaters shows that, if the filmmaker doesn't already have the movie closed captioned, then it's not up to the movie theater to provide devices for that particular movie. Of course, we never want to blame the messenger, which in this case, is the movie theater itself. It can be viewed as a disappointment for the lesser hearing, but it's also poor business management on the part of the filmmaker when they lose profits because lesser hearing patrons decide against seeing their movie without captioning. I am a strong advocate against such, and I have often written strong reviews to voice my concern, hoping that they will consider my disappointment in their poor business practices.

Practice self-love and operate in love...

Being at your best simply means always being able to practice self-love and to operate in love. How can we genuinely do what's best for others without love for ourselves in the rotation? My philosophy is that self-acceptance grows your *self-love*. This reaps endless benefits and joyful days for you and all of those around you. But first, we must tackle the awful wolf of self-acceptance inside of us. Like every person that we grow fond of, it all starts with our acceptance of them. There is no doubt that we each have had those experiences in life that we were tested to accept another person, whether it is being assigned a lab partner, working alongside an extremely talkative co-worker, or visiting a loathed family member.

This same acceptance goes for us—until we have enough consistent self-acceptance inside of us, then self-love is just an internal fight of the wolves. We fight ourselves when we mishear people. We fight ourselves when we answer incorrectly. We fight ourselves when asked a question that has already been asked. How about we adopt the slogan, "this too shall pass" and put those difficult moments behind us so that we can conquer self-love? What do I mean by this? Well, really, how close are you to self-love if you keep badgering yourself or feeling sorry for yourself every time you make a mistake.

Understand this, you are lesser hearing; this means that you are allowed to not hear some things correctly. What you are not allowed to do is sulk and sigh in it forever, refusing to get over it. This minimizes your self-love and doesn't let you be at your best.

The concept of acceptance is the same across the board, whether the acceptance is external or internal. Self-acceptance is essential, and I have found that we cannot even begin to accept others unless we have accepted ourselves. It is a far-reaching quality that we simply must vow to continually improve. How happy can you be for another person when you aren't satisfied with yourself entirely? As a hard of hearing person, I admit that sometimes I am not at peace with it, but I have learned not to allow it to cloud my happiness. It pops up and annoys me, but I refuse to let it have negative power in my life.

Without self-acceptance, your psychological well-being will suffer.

Consider an example: a young lady who refuses to attend weddings after planning her own that didn't happen. Yes, she is probably devastated, her feelings are hurt, and she simply refuses to face the emotions behind weddings—not wanting to watch others take vows when she never experienced her special day. Well, can you blame her? Many will probably side with her and understand this. Yet, what we don't realize is that the longer she takes to attend another wedding, she is living a woeful life—that she is not accepting a bad occasion in her life or letting that event pass.

The same goes for hearing loss. If we refuse to try socializing because we are getting frustrated, then we will eventually begin to live a sad woeful life. The best chance we have of conquering feelings of sadness is to challenge it to the point that it's just not bothersome anymore, and your psychological well-being becomes strengthened. Then, I can promise you that you have accepted yourself and are living at your best. Practicing self-love means saying to yourself, "I want to be a part of the conversation, and I will ask them to repeat it as often as necessary to stay in the conversation." When people see this, they will love your audacity and have no other choice but to repeat themselves. Never back down from telling people what you need, and then you will get what you need. That is exhibiting self-love.

My journey to self-acceptance

Some years ago, I decided to enroll in counseling at a local community outreach program in my area. A market crash had caused my real estate sales to decline drastically, and I had given up my teaching position a few years back. The economy and job market had declined as well and had hit me very hard. I lost my house, my car, my business tanked, and I filed for unemployment. At this time in my life, I could feel my overwhelming anxiety slowly becoming a depression, and adding fuel to the fire, I had just become a single mother. My counselor came to diagnose it as situational depression. This meant that a particular situation was bringing about depressive traits within me. I knew that the "situation" she was referring to in my diagnosis was my job searches. I had been out of work and job searching for an extended amount of time, and the searching, interviewing, and networking had taken a toll on my mental health.

"Deaf and hard-of-hearing people often face discriminatory hiring practices, employers' misconceptions, and barriers to job advancement. A study published in the *New York Times* in 2015 acknowledged that employers were thirty-four percent less likely to hire an experienced job candidate with a disability. Quite often, employers do not understand how to provide accessibility to people with different abilities, worrying that it will be arduous and costly." Oh boy, and did I realize this! It was a gruesome reality that I just couldn't hide from. I stressed about my job searches constantly and being hearing disabled didn't help. At least that's what I felt. That, sorry to say, was my non-acceptance of my hearing disability, and there were days for which I began to view my hearing loss as a burden. I had never felt this way about it before, and my spirit was really being tested. Day in and day out, I prayed and cried about not finding a job and being born with this terrible disability.

My friends and family eagerly reminded me of the beautiful person I was and the significant accomplishments that I had made. They thought that I was taking life too hard. *Taking life too hard*, I thought. *Well, they are not the one born with a hearing incompetency* was my answer. My actions were terrible during these days; I cried, sulked, and sighed everywhere. . . I was simply not good company. People began to get tired of me quickly, and I was draining everyone's energy around me. In fact, this is why I volunteered to be counseled so that I would have someone to talk to, because my own folks were done with me. I wreaked havoc and negativity with every person I spoke to. I just couldn't return to having a positive perspective on life.

I shied away from competing for certain jobs, and I even became unmotivated when others tried to offer opportunities to network. It was a valley that I would have to dig myself out of before the people in my life could feel any love from me again. My guidance counselor was amazing, though. She did a great job of allowing me to talk, vent, and express my feelings, and she shared with me the importance of giving people the space to be heard.

"A study by the National Institute on Deafness and Other Communication Disorders (NIDCD) shows that more than eleven percent of those with hearing loss also had depression, as opposed to only five percent in the general population. Depression was most prevalent in those between the ages of eighteen and sixty-nine." This is a large age gap, eighteen to sixty-nine, but I think that what this research shows is that those who suffer a hearing loss are often are two times more likely to become depressed, or experience depression at some point in their lives.

Understand it, conquer it, and move on

Venting is good, don't get me wrong, but too much venting is simply complaining. We have to be aware of this. Bless my counselor's heart for listening to the countless hours I spent complaining and mocking myself. This was a time when I was so impatient and reactive to everyone and everything around me. My heart was unsettled because there were a lot of unsettled ways festering within me.

One day, I had a good friend over to my new place to help me with yard work. It was a beautiful afternoon, and Rodney had just finished mowing the lawn. Good weather always relaxed me, so it was the perfect day to receive what he was trying to tell me. We began talking about our shared spiritual walk, and he shared with me a book called "Purification of the Heart."

Rodney and I always had uplifting talks, and I valued his advice. Incredibly, I hadn't realized how long I had allowed this painful, negative energy to grow and fester within me. "Purification of the Heart" was a book that immensely defined the different negative energies that we allow into our lives, such as hate, anger, and jealousy. I was also reading a few other books at that time, and they helped me view life from the eyes of others, which was enlightening for me.

Reading more about these negative energies, such as anger and shame, allowed me to pinpoint—and call out—my jealousy and anger. When I continued to see them physically as words written down in a book repeatedly, being defined, broken down, and analyzed, I was able to honestly decide whether I exhibited what was being shared. This is what helped to move me out of my situational depression. Yes, my counselor let me sit there and talk forever, but it was when I decided to pick up a book, read, and understand that I began accepting myself again. Books are not people; they can be useful tools if we tend to take conversations with others too personally.

My counselor, books, and meditation practices helped me out of depression. I read about anger, hate, disappointment, shame, and jealousy (among many other terms) and decided to tame down the fire in me when I realized that it was only blocking my success and relationships. I always shared my resources with my counselor, and when I told her that I no longer needed her services, she diagnosed me as cured. She needed to hear it from me. She didn't rush me through the process, and this is what I needed to come to this decision on my own, not to be told.

After a while, I just knew that I had placed the past behind me. We completed questionnaires about how I felt about my life with my entirely new perspective. I sometimes wonder what would have happened if I had not spent my time reading and learning about my heart and what I was going through. Wow, again, the power of books.

How hearing aids improve your life

Self-acceptance means that you have accepted your hearing aids as beneficial, and you know they have the power to improve your life! So now, let's talk about how these devices enhance our lives and make us better people. Yes, if you love yourself and want what's best for you, then this is a no-brainer; in fact, it's something that I would dare not leave out of this book. Starkey, a hearing aid vendor, says that hearing aids improve your life by giving you the following:

- Ease in communication
- Intimacy and warmth in family relationships
- Communication in relationships
- Earning power
- Sense of control over your life
- Social participation
- Emotional stability

With all of these pointers, we have either started to discuss them, or we will address them in this book. I just wanted to give a few listed positives because this list should be your greatest joy in wearing a hearing aid. Yes, find joy in the fact that you will be empowered by wearing it; you can participate socially, and gain better control over your life when you are wearing it. You are investing in the quality of your life. You are taking your power back, and now, the next step in conquering this is simply saying to others, "accept me as I am."

There is a sense of connection that comes from wearing a hearing aid, so when you refuse to wear it, your tendencies to connect with others will decrease, and your likelihood of pursuing isolation will increase. With hearing aids, you will stay on top of your game and remain sharp because you are investing in yourself.

Know what you want and go after it...

In researching for this book, I revisited a bestselling book that I had read a year ago, "Secrets of the Millionaire Mind," written by T. Harv Ecker. One of my most memorable phrases read was, "The number one reason most people don't get what they want is because they don't know what they want."

When I read this book, I realized that I had never stopped to analyze what job I felt comfortable performing as a hearing disabled worker. I had always only analyzed those jobs that I couldn't do. What a mindset, right? And what I didn't know was that reading this one statement would help me get a handle on my life, drive me to understand my skill set at the level of severely disabled, lift my self-acceptance, and enable me to feel better about my job searches. Wow, the power of reading for knowledge. All it took was for me to open the book instead of continuous self-questioning.

Let's just be real here… no one's going to accept within you that which you do not accept within yourself. If you mope and complain about your hearing loss, then people will do the same. Not that they feel that way, but they will just assume that this is your way of dealing with it. A poor way of dealing with it, if I might say. Throughout the year of recovering from depression, I learned that my strongest qualities were writing, educating, leading, and coaching others. I had tried the real estate sales profession for years, but my evolving passion for teaching my clients always stood in the way of getting more sales. I was overcommitted to client satisfaction, and as a result, I was refusing to work with too many just to please the few that I was working exclusively with.

I wanted to teach them how to choose the best inspector, read the fine print of a contract, and analyze the value of the home they wanted. They were always encouraged to purchase the house that was most suitable to their needs, but I couldn't quite grasp the "we have to quickly write today and get you closed, because I have other clients" pitch, which was used by many agents to stay on top of the industry and make a lot of money.

Chasing money and deals is a necessary skill as an agent, but that was not my passion. Nevertheless, through understanding self-love, I had figured out what my passion and gifts were. From that point on, I wrote continuously about what was important to me and searched for jobs that would provide me with favorable skills. I also continued my decision to begin intense reading again to educate myself. I created a booklist and started my venture back into reading, for mind control and happiness. I was out of the valley of depression and marveling in self-acceptance, assured in my ways.

Reading to pave the way for love

As I expressed earlier, my childhood books removed me from my harsh reality of missing much that was communicated around me. And in my adult life, once again, a story or self-help advice from a book had disconnected me from my reality for a while. It was similar to turning my life off and escaping to someone else's world. Who knows, maybe I needed this disconnection in my adult life, too. Many might argue that this is a sure way of running from problems, but I beg to differ when it comes to the lesser hearing. What joy we feel when there is no struggle in communicating, when the entire conversation can be received and enjoyed, or when a joke is not missed. Sheer joy, I will tell you that. It's the same as someone who has poor vision, but loves the audible app; it is without struggle, and that is always good.

Books are an involuntary practice of mind control, awareness, and articulation. If you can begin to create thoughts, visions, and imagery for what you are reading, then your conscious mind can rest for a while. Did you know that experts estimate that the mind thinks between 60,000-80,000 thoughts per day? Wow! Hold on! That's an average of 2,500-3,300 thoughts per hour. The mind is incredible. My point is that reading and controlling my thoughts has propelled me to a calmer, paced world; to a peaceful environment of self-acceptance, where I began slowly to rebuild my internal love for myself through reading.

Why am I sharing this? It's quite simple: So that you will know that the habit of "getting stuck" in life is a natural part of life. Many times in life, you will figure things out along the way, and if no one has ever told you that, please take heed to my suggestion. Being hearing disabled can cause us to overthink, but life is not meant to be that hard. You have to believe that you simply deserve a good life just as much as the next person. That is self-love in its purest form. This means you have to continue to do what is right for you, letting your light shine.

Disconnect and meditate from time to time

By feeling the disconnection and meditating from life from time to time, you will calmly begin to think about whatever your gift is. Take a few "What is my gift?" quizzes online, confirm your passion, and work from there. Fifteen years of real estate work never brought me as much happiness as speaking at events, coaching, or writing a book. In life, it is important that we are able to do what's second nature to us. This will allow your body to receive more positive energy and self-love. It will also allow for joyful experiences of passion as you embark upon your gift. And finally, the greatest benefit of all is the "ultimate biological vitamin superpower," which will contribute to your extended life span and increased livelihood.

Beautiful self-love vs. ugly arrogance

Self-love overpowers that sad wolf inside of you that hesitated to speak up when you needed something. "Yes, full house! I've got the internal esteem to know that what I need is important. I have learned to accept and love myself, and there's nothing you can do about it!" Well, I will kind of pipe down for a minute and just throw out there that, in no way am I implying arrogance.

Arrogance involves a problematic behavior in which a person continually boasts of themselves. To have absolutely no humility is also to be outright arrogant. Humility should always be sought out, simply because we just cannot always be correct. If we honor and practice humility, then we brace ourselves to accept that another's approach may sometimes be the better approach. Just be sure that you're not practicing arrogance. Arrogance works against love, taking away the ability to love. It comes with the ugly stench of entitlement, which no person or group wants to be subjected to.

> "Be completely humble and gentle; be patient, bearing with one another in love."—Ephesians 4:2

So, now that we have vowed not to practice the ugly arrogance (for it doesn't make us better people), let's get back to the self-love concept so that we can embrace it. Self-love is merely having a high regard for one's own happiness and well-being. When we build our self-love, we can become better at accepting adversity because nothing is as bothersome. We stand in long customer service lines without pouting, because in our minds, we are saying, "It has been a good day."

Love is a tense feeling of affection, and therefore, self-love is an intense feeling of affection towards oneself. It often becomes an unintended protective shield. With this protective shield, our intense feeling of love for ourselves is refusing the view beyond it; we are embracing challenges and not holding the opinions of others so firmly to our hearts anymore. When self-love arises in us, we become less critical of others; the rejection of others will become less meaningful. All of these things make for an easier life.

Be more conscious of what's right for you.

Well, as a good friend told me last week, "We are in a conscious time." I couldn't agree more. We are in a time where people are more conscious of what's right for them, a time in which they are aware of the ingredients being cooked into their foods, or what benefits the latest yoga class offers. It's always better to be more conscious of what's happening around us, but the question is… are you practicing what's good for you, or waiting for the right time? That's a reasonable question. Do you know why? Well, because most people reading this book can say they practice self-love, but they sometimes struggle with self-acceptance. Or, they may say that they practice self-love, but don't really implement it in their lives; it's just a feeling. Well, love is a feeling, but it's much more than that.

Love of self, when implemented, goes a step further. When we apply self-love in our lives, we make healthier food choices, adding them to our diet. We sign up and attend the yoga class.

The next step after learning anything should be implementation… applying what we have learned. Okay, so I have learned this. How do I use it? This is where our internal drive steps on the gas to get us to the gym, or in the direction of the vegetables and healthier foods in the grocery store. What people have to understand is that every decision we make begins internally; the stronger your love of self, the higher likelihood of doing what's best for you.

Hearing Loss down the Family Line

One thing that I truly love about my upbringing is that I was raised in a household where the lesser hearing habits were accepted and familiar. Thankfully, I can say that I never felt unloved or unlovable in my childhood. My dad (who has hearing loss) was my first emotional and psychological coach, giving me the clarity and structure, I needed. He always reiterated that hearing loss was a physical disability, but it had nothing to do with my ability to learn. He also showed me how to take my time washing a car, using the right water (at the right temperature), and not using cheap clothes or cheap soap, which according to him, can leave scratches.

My mom was an excellent caretaker. She kept up with my hearing aids, making sure that they were maintained and available—telling me not to put them on wet sinks or in the pockets of my jeans. She allowed me to assist her in cooking and grocery shopping, showing me the best brands of food to buy, and how to measure portions when cooking for a large family. Pretty soon, I was making dinner as a teen and washing the cars on occasional weekends.

I was also blessed to have a cousin, Brenda Johnson, as my Speech Therapist throughout elementary school; it was a great start in my early education years and a service I needed to strengthen my articulation and pronunciation skills. Brenda was a second cousin on my Dad's side of the family. I always appreciated her presence, but I didn't favor her reason (speech services) when she stopped past the classroom to take me to her office. I felt like a special needs child, not at all how I felt at home. It was accepted at home. Here in her office, it seemed like "I had a problem." I think she picked up on this. She would give me cookies and potato chips from her lunch bag and always came with a smile, happy to teach me how to enunciate when I spoke. She said, "Dominique, I need you to pronounce your words more clearly," or "Place your tongue inside for the letters." Then she showed me how to pronounce the letter and ask me to repeat the words, using words with the letter in it.

It was a blessing, since I could not always hear myself pronounce the words. I like to think that it definitely contributed to my excellent lip-reading skills, as well. Although tiring for my mind at times, her cheerful personality kept me motivated. She was a significant part of my journey to self-acceptance. We read books and described pictures. We listened to tapes and articulated sounds. We even held good conversations to stay afloat of my social skills. She allowed me to express my thoughts and waited for me to formulate those thoughts correctly.

From time to time, in her care, I sometimes felt (in my earlier years) that something was internally wrong with me. It was confusing for me as a child. I didn't know why I needed those services, and sometimes, it made me sad. Yet, I would later learn that this was so far from the truth. Having her there enabled me to see that this was not the case. I, now, better understand her role, but as a child, it was not very clear why I had to be singled out.

I currently have two sisters who are both Speech Therapists, and I'm able to understand many benefits of their services. Overall, speech therapy can have a wide range of benefits that you may not even realize. These include:

- Developing conversational skills to improve interactions with others.
- Expressing thoughts, ideas, and needs in a more understandable way.
- Self-regulation and following rules for conversation.
- Social appropriateness in various settings and situations.
- Improved articulation so others can understand what you are saying.
- Non-verbal communication skills, such as facial expressions or body language.
- Putting together words in a sentence that make sense.
- Understanding the meaning of more words and how to use them.
- Using alternative communication devices, such as picture exchange communication systems or text-to-speech programs.

"Starting speech therapy early can help to address problems before they become more serious. This can help your child to be more successful in school, build their self-esteem, and become a more independent communicator." (2) [5]

I couldn't agree more with this statement, as I researched the work of a speech pathologist; that is why I decided to share it. My speech pathologist enabled me to have more confident and meaningful conversations among my family, peers, and teachers. My childhood, as I described it, was of a child with wondering questions. So even in school, I wondered. In class, I wondered. I wondered, *did people hear what I said?* I wondered, *am I talking too loudly?* There were so many unanswered questions that could have added to my insecurities, had my speech pathologist not been there. She was a significant blessing—lessening my tendency for mind roaming, enabling me to focus on my schoolwork, and improving my articulation skills.

So, let's fast forward to my adult life. Articulation (deciphering sounds correctly) has made me the great presenter that I am today. I am the first to give a toast at family events or volunteer to read the next selection in a reading group. I love giving business presentations, teaching a group of people, or even sharing a poem that I wrote with an audience. In no way has this stopped me from achieving the great skills in reading and presenting, so that words are clear, easily understood, and interpreted by others! Hooray! Hooray for you, too, if you've got the power of excellent articulation. Yes, presenting is confidence-building, but first, you have to be assured that you are reading well. That is self-love in another form, assurance in self.

The love and acceptance of our hearing loss were so clear and present in my family that it would be foolish to stand around mad and upset about it, while everyone joked about it. My uncle and his family (my cousins) loved to make jokes and have fun. We played tricks on each other, hid hearing aids, and even muted the TV a lot, just to mess with each other. We had loud conversations and then "go low," just to mess with each other.

We were a mess, but we loved each other. It helped me to shake the dust off and keep moving. It enabled me to step out of my shell of life sometimes and stop taking things so personally. I think that, in my family, I probably took it more personally than anybody. God forbid I lost a hearing aid; it would be a sad and overwhelming day for me. But not my cousins; if they lost a hearing aid, they would try and hide it from my aunt and uncle for a while, only to be caught later. They took so many risks and just clearly never took the loss to heart as I did.

Life is what you make it...

By sharing my family history and our dorky stories, I'm saying that "life is what you make it." Laughter and good energy have to be made, self-love has to be made, and self-acceptance has to be made. Self-acceptance is important because, as I said before, if you are annoyed by your hearing loss, then other people will be annoyed for you. Here's a thought! How you present it is how others will receive it! I am both extremely thankful for these cousins in my life and proud of them.

We were recently planning a large 65th birthday event via group text (for my dad and uncle who are twins) a few months ago, and there they were, in the family text feed, throwing out "hearing" jokes. It's life; you have to laugh. Better yet, you better laugh. "As it turns out, the human brain is wired to respond positively to laughter and your smile, which is generating feel good chemicals, and this can be of great help for depression. The wind of the mind is so strong that the brain responds, even when we smile at ourselves in the mirror, or stimulate laughter and enthusiasm." (3)[6]

I remember when I chose to convert my natural colored hearing aid mold to a plum-violet colored one. It was awesome! It was at a time in my life when I was branding myself and "creating my hype," as my social media coach called it. In real estate, branding was used to set us apart from our competition. I marketed my business in the Washington, D.C. and Maryland area, so the competition was fierce.

Branding was a personalized concept that we adopted for marketing, used for Facebook and Instagram posts, Canvas Creations, digital media marketing, gifs, logos, professional photography, and more. I loved the hype that I was creating, so I decided to go all-in with my business. It was the time that people would see me marvel in being hearing impaired.

It seemed like the thing to do; I was fascinated by the pretty colors that hearing aid molds came in. When I first began to wear it, I was a bit skeptical, but that was only for one day. I had chosen it because it was beautiful in the catalog at my audiologist's office. I was smitten with it once I saw it, and knew I was not putting it back. I chose to go shopping on this very day to put myself out there for prospective likes in the real world, not just on social media.

My social media followers loved it, and so did bystanders at the mall. I received so many compliments that day. It attracted so many great vibes; people were astonished, as it was something that many had yet to see. I was beyond surprised, happily realizing the day and age that we are in. I have a saying for this time: "Do as you like." That's the advice that I want to give you now, as we talk about the visual humans around you. People gravitate to those who take chances, like wearing the colorful hearing aid that they like. I have never been able to find a tattoo that I identify with (and I have none), but this colorful mold was a no-brainer. My thoughts were, *people are going to look anyway. Well, let them be amazed.*

This colored mold sets the mode for the type of person that I am before people talk to me. It shows people that I wear my hearing aid with pride. I'm a lady. I like a colorful purse, beautiful lipstick colors, a cute cell phone case, and a pretty plum hearing aid mold. It was, and still is, the prettiest hearing aid I had ever seen. My dad loves it whenever I match jewelry and makeup to it; he always compliments me.

People are incredibly visual nowadays, and they are daring as well, and employers are starting to gravitate towards this. In networking, my colorful hearing aid is a great conversation starter, just like a beautiful pair of shiny glasses. People have come to accept that it's how you wear it that sells itself. Wearing it with pride gives haters a few more drops of insecurities, since they're already insecure anyway, and it provides the confident one a reason to admire you.

It's like indirectly saying, "Yes, you may be confident in your own way, but could you rock a colored hearing aid, if you were me?" Just a thought. Not intending any pun, but what did Beyoncé make? That's right... lemonade! When life gives you lemons, you make lemonade, and people love you for it. You take the glimpses and stares, the oohs and the ahhhs, and make your connections. You talk to people willingly about it with no guards up and proclaim that you are a solidified person who loves being that way. That, too, is self-love at its finest. These are people who are smitten by your energy; they love your drive, your persona, your daring.

Many people gravitate towards this right now because being different or daring sells quickly. I learned this years ago while making social media videos on YouTube, Facebook, and Instagram. People marveled at the videos that I made; I was comical, venturesome, and live! They marvel when you share your personal story as I did for many days on social media. It wins likes and followers, but in the long run, it may land you your dream job or cause a potential employer to ring your phone. I'm not saying that the colored hearing aid is for everyone; I'm saying that wearing it with confidence and pride matters, how people receive you matters, and your willingness to share confidently matters. It's a big step, but by the end of this book, I promise that you will be able to face your biggest fears and challenges confidently.

Visuals elicit emotions

"Visual inputs generate emotion in us. And if there is something that our brain loves more than images, it's emotion. Emotions, and how the brain processes them, make us feel, react and survive. We are always on the lookout for visuals because they generate emotions, and emotions create deep connection. In fact, images can elicit any range of feelings, from awe to amusement, to sadness and that emotion doesn't have to "Mr. Positive" to create a connection. Emotions help us survive, thrive, make better decisions, and understand our surroundings." (4) [7]

What does all of this mean? It means that when many people see the hearing aid visually, it may draw upon an emotion. The emotion may be good or bad, but it's up to you, and it's the energy you give to select how the conversation will go. For instance, someone walks up to you and says, "OMG, Sheila didn't tell me that you wore a hearing aid. Will you be able to hear, okay?" You have two ways to go—*steer* or *clear* this conversation. First, you could respond by saying, "Girl, Sheila has known about this forever. My hearing aid is my true BFF (best friend forever), so we make a lot of things happen together." This steers the conversation to their amazement at your energy. Or, you could clear the conversation by saying something like: "Yes. It's been with me since birth and… I mean, I deal with it." This brings forth negative emotions from others that you want to avoid.

Simply put, your energy has to be right for you to make a deep connection. It has to be genuine and not forced or coerced. This is when the self-love factor kicks in, yet again.

Since people are visual and more forthright now, we have to be ready, more than ever, to answer those awkward questions, yet, at the same time, try to refrain from bringing the wrong energy into the conversation, which makes it more awkward. You can never go wrong with the "confident woman hair flip" for the ladies, or the "what's up" head nod for the guys.

I do this all of the time, and it works. Better yet, come back strong so that they stop asking so many questions. The shy, pushover person will be mocked. But the fierce, confident person will answer your question, thank you for the conversation, and move on.

SECTION II

What You Need to Change

Lead Page II:
Change is Good

CHANGE HAPPENS EVERY DAY: A new hairstyle, a new friend, a new hobby. However, the change that we'll address in this section is massive, and with it being huge, it will be sure to exert a much more intense lifestyle that you are going to love! Are you ready for this? We're going to shake up your world and conquer your biggest fears that go with being hard of hearing! That's the change that I am talking about!

If you are reading this book, then maybe, just maybe, you need to be more effective in your life. What do I mean by that? Increasing effectiveness in our lives happens when we find our lost motivation and take action to achieve what we set out to do; as a result of this, we achieve change. In a nutshell, positive change means increasing the flow of productivity and motivation in our lives to advance forward. A 'zest for success' is what I would call it, and with it we push for change so that we may be more effective in every area of our lives.

> *"Effectiveness in life does not come from focusing on what is automatic, easy, or natural for us. Rather, it is the result of how we consciously strive to meet life's harder challenges, grow beyond our comforts, and deliberately work to overcome our biases and*

> *preferences, so that we may understand, love, serve, and lead others."* –Brendon Burchard (2) [1]

There is always a time when we will have to acknowledge and challenge this need to be better in our lives. Why? Because none of us were born with the habits that allow us to always be at our best. Especially when we have to adjust to lesser hearing every minute of our lives.

These habits are learned, practiced, and monitored; and they grow, based on our willingness to change: Change from learned lifestyle habits. Change from negative work habits. Change from toxic relationship habits. Change from low quality conversation habits. There are many other areas that we could address throughout our lives, but within the scope of this book, we will look at change in five major areas. We will discover a practice of:

1. Changing how we relate to others socially.
2. Changing how we relate in our careers and on the job.
3. Changing how we relate in our personal relationships.
4. Recognizing and changing what works against our ability to practice great self-love.
5. Finally understanding how great conversations evolve.

I am super excited to share this with you, as I have seen all of these five areas of my life evolve through careful thought and optimism. Let's get started!

CHAPTER 4

Create Your Self-Awareness Hype...
Change How You Relate to Others!

> *"Life is a daring adventure or nothing at all."*
> -Helen Keller, Hearing Disabled Author

To be great at socializing and getting along, you must first understand what is expected of you. To be more open and understanding of what is expected of you, you must be aware of your likes and dislikes. This creates, internally, a strong sense of identity. When you know what you like, there are not many moments to ponder or self-question; thus, you can present yourself best when relating to others. One sure black and white way to determine what type of socializer you are is to realize whether you are an extrovert or an introvert.

Living as an introvert
with an extrovert soul doesn't last.

This statement may seem confusing at first, but I am implying that there is confusion when we think we are one way, but we live as something else. Not everyone can so quickly determine whether they are an introvert or extrovert. The big difference between the two can be answered by asking yourself the question: *How do you gain energy?* If you gain energy from doing things alone, you're an introvert, while on the flip side, if you gain energy from large crowds of people, then you're an extrovert. Figuring this out has been a struggle in my own life. When we look at these two traits, sometimes it may take on a plight of self-discovery to understand which suits you best and ensures your happiness. The truth is that no one wants to be alone all of the time, and no one wants to be surrounded by people all of the time. That's a broad stretch; however, your tendencies can show you exactly how far the pendulum swings for you and to which trait.

Introverts find happiness internally while extroverts do the opposite—finding happiness externally. How do we accomplish that? Well, this is a matter of what activities you enjoy. Do you enjoy going to a one hundred and twenty-seat movie theater, or is a night at home, watching Netflix enough? Do you start to feel tired and worn out quickly around large groups of people, or does a good crowd boost your energy? Or, even a more straightforward question: Do you prefer time alone as opposed to spending time in the company of others? Think about the last few outings that you have been invited to. Did you decline, and if so, why?

I will admit, I am not fond of water parks. You know the drill if you are hearing disabled. First, you have to figure out what you're going to wear to protect your hearing aid from the "water monster of wetness" that's dreadfully covering every inch of the park. Second, God forbid your device does get wet while you're there; well, that would just ruin your day. But how would you fix it immediately? Do you have the patience to wait for your aid to dry out? And third, will you find yourself walking in a crowd after a water ride, unable to hear and participate in the conversation because your hearing aid is safely put away to avoid getting wet again? It's a gruesome predicament that many normal hearing people don't really understand.

Sheesh! Did you see how quickly I just named three compelling reasons not to visit a water park? Yet, I will be honest... I love the rides at water parks. Every single water park ride I have ever tried, I have truly enjoyed. Yet, to this day, if you ask me to accompany you to a waterpark, I will probably leave you on your own. There you have it, a prime example of foregoing fun events to avoid handling your emotions.

The concept that I'm sharing, however, is much bigger than water parks. It's about identifying with one or the other. Although I have enjoyed a few extrovert events, I often identify with an introvert because of my avid reading and deep-thinking habits, or because I prefer time alone. I would probably choose to stay home, and Netflix binge over going to a water park. I admit that my hearing loss tends to make me negatively regress, making my extroverted needs less of a priority. That regression, in turn, gives me the desire to stay home and not fulfill my socializing needs.

We have to know what activities we prefer, so that we aren't discouraged by our disabilities, and regretful later when we have missed beautiful memories with friends and family.

Don't Block Your Blessings.

I like to call it "blocking myself" or even "blocking my blessings." This can happen when you are so distracted by having to struggle with conversations that you miss out on meeting great people—people who could change your life. Just think about what I would have missed if I had decided to decline the chance to meet Bill Clinton while in high school. That experience, and his image, stayed in my mind throughout my college years as encouragement; it helped me understand how capable I was.

One way that you may identify with being an introvert is that you write everything down. This is me. Where would I be without my pen and paper? Years ago, as people took to electronic planners and notepads, I was bothered and worried that society would leave pen and paper. I was baffled and was sprung with joy every time I bought a new notebook in a stationery store. Aside from the struggle of accepting electronics, I learned that my need to write everything down was here to stay; I was simply less productive without it.

Introverts Tend to Overthink

Writing down thoughts, dates, events, reminders, and notes (whether with pens and paper or digital) helps us clear our minds and make way to think of other things. This is particularly helpful to an introvert because we are always thinking on and on and on. There is nothing wrong with extensive thinking. It is only when it becomes overthinking, worry, or anxiety that it begins to bring us to absurdity.

In other words, use the pen and paper to write, but set your limit. There are actually times when I say to myself, "No, I don't have to write that down." It gives me a sense of control. And of course, we have no sense of control when we don't possess the ability to control how much we write down. When we have too many notes, reminders, and events, we have to go back, reorganize, and rethink why we wrote it in the first place. This is a loss of time; when we see this habit develop in our lives, we will count it against ourselves as a fault. It's a known fact that too much of anything is not good, just as too much "writing it down" is definitely not good. Learn to put the pen and paper down and trust yourself.

Another known fact about introverts is that they tend to avoid large crowds and prefer smaller groups. There is absolutely nothing wrong with this preference; however, my advice would be to make sure that you're able to adjust, so that you can still hear if the event is moved to a larger area or you accidentally misread the number of attendees. This is life; it's very fast-paced and competitive. There is no time to leave an event simply because it's just too large. No, these are the times that we are in. We must simply stop and adjust. Believe me, I have left many wonderful events… and a word to the wise, that never goes in your favor.

A few years ago, I attended a woman's conference at my church. I had planned for weeks in advance to attend; it was going to be awesome! I arrived at the event, and the hostesses greeted every participant with beautiful gift bags. I mingled with a few choir friends beforehand, took my seat, and was all set. The program began, and the crowd stood for the opening song. Everything was just lovely until they decided to convert the stage to a "living room" setup. It was supposed to convey a type of "sister circle" setup. I was beyond frustrated and concerned that the circle now seemed so much further from the stage. I was astonished and terribly disappointed.

Never Let Your Emotions Decide for You

I would like to say that I tried to hear, but I really didn't try at all. In my mind, I panicked. "How was I supposed to hear this?" "Oh, people could be so rude sometimes," were the thoughts that ran through my mind. I said goodbye to my church sisters quickly and left the sanctuary. I was disappointed. I didn't make it to my car, but stopped in the hallway and cried. This was my church, and I loved it here. "Would other events be like this one?" I thought to myself. An usher saw me in the hall sobbing and asked me to please share what was wrong. I told her my situation and that I could not hear much of the presentation. She was saddened for me. There was not much that she could do, except to offer me a few words of sympathy. I left the event and was upset with myself for the rest of the day. I had really let myself down.

I later emailed member services with my concerns. My point is that I allowed my emotions to take over my ability to hear anything at all. When I left the event, I hadn't received anything from the presentation, but there were steps that I could have taken. Sometimes, we cannot avoid large groups; work or even family events may require us to adjust. Regardless, you have to have a few ideas up your sleeve to combat this—as I have shared in Chapter 2.

The Good Introvert Habit

There is one peculiar thing about introverts and their feelings that I must point out. Their alone time is very much preferred, and it is viewed as a time to replenish themselves. In other words, they enjoy periods of solitude. I tend to pursue this a lot, as my daughter converses a lot. However, with this gesture, I'm going to encourage it. I would not ask that you adjust this habit. I find alone time to be very beneficial, especially for one that carries a hearing loss.

As I look back over my life, I know that my alone time helps keep me calm and composed. I will admit that I tend to feel misunderstood, but the truth is that I'm the only one that needs to be comfortable with it. Only I need to understand it to be efficient. Of course, I am much more comfortable when others can adjust, but not everyone does, do they? I have learned that it is not our duty in life to understand the lives of others and vice versa. However, it is a great justice to understand ourselves; this alone time should be extremely helpful to those who give it a try.

Mark Your Calendar for Solitude

If you have a busy life, I encourage you to mark your calendar for solitude time; this can be done in twenty to thirty-minute spurts, or a full hour, if time permits. Use your lunch hour or rise early. Solitude is what reboots your brain. It improves concentration and productivity. Living in a low-volume world requires a lot of concentration and brainpower, so why not stop at times to tune the world out and unwind? That's what alone time does for us. When you try it, you will find that it also helps you through your problems more effectively. This also allows you to avoid working when you're distracted by incoming information. My biggest distraction is emails. I can take a few texts here and there, but email notifications just cannot pop up on my phone or iPad. It's amazing how your mind can be in full power work mode, and then you receive an email that swallows up all of your attention, setting you back an hour or two—been there, done that. I have made it a duty of mine not to handle extra tasks during prioritized moments.

Introverts probably would prefer emails over phone conversations, though. Of course, I would prefer to use my eyes over my ears any day. Small habits, such as this one, are wise to take on with a hearing loss, even though they are introvert preferences; they can favor your progress and lifestyle. You will also find that solitude can enhance your relationship with others because when you've stepped away for some alone time to sit and reflect, you can more easily listen to the concerns of others; this is what life is all about. It's about building relationships.

What many don't realize is that solitude is a great way to touch on your creative side. It allows you to think deeply in quiet times. I used to hop, skip, and jump, on the go everywhere, when I first became a mother. I would rush to work, rush to pick up my daughter, and rush home to cook dinner. I rushed with every fiber of my being, all day long. The only quiet time I had was during the night hours. What a shame that was. When my daughter turned six years old, she became a little more independent. We started to relax more around the house; we began to do what I liked at times and to do what she liked at other times. She shared her patterned coloring books and coloring pencils with me. I spent a Sunday afternoon coloring with her.

Pretty soon, I bought my own patterned coloring book with pictures and a set of pencils. I colored on my own time when she visited relatives, or late at night when she was asleep. I started to see that it was the perfect way to start the week. On Sunday, I could get a mental grip on what was happening for the upcoming week while remaining in a relaxed state. I was not frustrated, rushed, or panicked. It gave me time to think over a lot of my thoughts.

I will say, it was much more productive than stopping in between laundry loads and saying to myself, "What do I have to do this week?" That was simply not a time where thoughts were flowing. One of the most exceptional words of advice given to me as a real estate agent was, "Dominique, never try to multi-task." I stand by that to this day, and now, I simply prioritize my life, making times of solitude for myself.

Introverts Think Before They Speak

Aside from avoiding large groups and the need for solitude, introverts also tend to think before they speak. If there was never a more used quote from parent to child to "think before you speak." When I say that they think before they speak, I mean that they are careful with their words; they are deep thinkers, so they usually muddle over a situation before they arrive at a conclusion. This is a major accomplishment of mine. I didn't always practice this. I will admit that it probably came about as a result of years of withdrawal—years of withdrawal that I wouldn't want others to have to experience. Take this as a cue to make time for yourself so that you have thought through things; so that people can receive you as more empathetic. Thinking before you speak is a good thing.

No matter how you have to learn it, everyone deserves for you to think before you speak. Imagine the world we would live in if no one did this, and how chaotic that would be. That's what makes this concept so very important. I have always said that if you want to know the value of something, try taking it out of your life for a while. Take the concept of speaking too quickly out of your life; I can assure you that you will not miss it.

I love my friends and family who choose to think before they speak. It's very enlightening; these people are more pleasant to talk to and hold conversations with than others. But it doesn't come easy. It takes patience and thoughtfulness. It's practiced by people that take the time to think about others when they are not around. These people prepare for when they will see others again. It should usually be the actions of a good close friend. They say, "I'm going to tell her when I see her not to be worried about her situation," or "Can't wait to see him and say how proud I am of him." This is a trait, too, that can be rather useful for one with a hearing disability.

This ability to think before we speak will help us have good conversations when we have missed something. Or, some people may call it "saving face."

How is that so? Let's say you're at a friend's happy hour birthday party and he asks you a question, just to make small talk. You don't quite hear him over the loud music. So, he shouts it out, only for you to miss it again. He's beginning to look a little frustrated, but you don't want his mood to change at his party; besides, he's such a good friend. Well, you thought of him yesterday and remembered the awesome trip his mother took him on for his last birthday.

So, instead of answering the question, you say, "Oh, don't worry about it. Hey, I meant to tell you that what your mom did for your birthday last year was wonderful. That must have been awesome." Believe me, now the small talk question is out the window. Some people may look at this as "changing the subject," and that may not always be a good thing. Some people prefer us to continue to tell them that we did not hear them, but this can be very stressful. A good friend should understand that we mean well and that stressing to hear at a certain point will only lead to increased frustration after many attempts. However, in this case, you are quickly telling him that you didn't hear him. He is feeling flattered and extra special that you remembered. This is what people who are careful with their words do for us. They think of us and plan how they will talk with us. It's a great effort to building relationships because people love flattery.

Small Circles vs. Large Circles...

Finally, introverts tend to keep small circles of friends because they tend to "think" of others immensely. I am very particular about my circle of friends. Everyone in it serves a purpose in my life, as I do in theirs. I talk more about building and expanding this great circle in Chapter 9.

Extroverts, on the other hand, tend to be viewed as attention seekers because of their enthusiasm. However, I couldn't be prouder of an extrovert that is hearing disabled; if this is you, then you rock! Kudos! I'm so serious! It can be challenging to be enthusiastic, with thoughts of your hearing disability in your head everywhere you go. This is why I will again say to work hard at understanding what your likes and dislikes are. If you're a born extrovert, then you don't want your hearing to change this. Being able to be the life of the party or socializing among an array of people is an impressive skill that shouldn't be taken for granted.

Personally, I love the extrovert's spontaneous ways. My only advice with this trait would be to slow down and think carefully. If you hate being alone, as some extroverts do, then just remember that having people around for validation is great, but it will be extremely difficult for you to have quality time for yourself this way. You will have to intentionally set aside time for self-assessment, which can be an outright headache for extroverts.

They may think, "You want me to plan for my own alone time when I love the company of people? Really? No, thanks." But truthfully, everyone does need some alone time. In fact, quality time for self has proven to be one of the most vital steps taken by millionaires. Overindulging yourself in loud, crowded environments often, or too much, can be extremely detrimental to your mental well-being. Slow down and make time for yourself and watch your life excel.

Talking to a brick wall

Also, be mindful of the fact that opening up and talking with too many people about your problems (which extroverts tend to do) may begin to make some people assume that your hearing loss is what may be causing your problems. In this case, it can start to feel like talking to a brick wall because they simply don't understand your capabilities. No pun intended, just giving you the scoop and calling it as I see it. The world does have its share of shallow-minded people.

These shallows sometimes assume that we aren't handling our hearing loss well. They don't know that we function just fine on our own. They say things like, "Oh yeah, she goes through a lot with her hearing loss, so maybe that's the real problem." "No, that's not my problem, but you are," is what I would tell them. I'm cracking myself up on that one. But again, maybe they weren't worth opening up to in the first place. This is exactly my point… people who listen to your problems have to be ready to accept what you are stating as your problem as a fact and nothing else.

Simply put, they must believe in you and your capabilities, or as I said, it will be just talking to a brick wall. You can accomplish more by screening who you tell what. Fewer friends, in my opinion, means more intimate relationships; and only within these close relationships will you be taking less of a risk when you share your life and dilemmas.

My mom is a great extrovert. Even in writing this book and talking about extroverts, she pops into my mind. She is always somewhere different with a different friend, or group of friends. A social butterfly, she is always meeting a new friend. I love it for her, but myself… I'm a little more resistant to so many people. I believe that the desire to be too friendly and eager to know too many people can get you in a world of trouble. Regardless of the severity of your hearing loss, the people that you associate with have to be open-minded enough to accommodate that loss. Wow, I really sound like a true introvert right now. But I'm being brutally honest here, and my point is valid. Those friends who don't make waves and accept you are indeed valuable.

Have Your Fun

I do have a few extrovert traits, though. For instance, one of them is the love for dancing. If dancing makes me happy, it will lift my confidence when I'm able to do it. I sing along, bend, twist, and shake confidently, loving every moment, while inside of me, my ego is soaring through the roof. Now, let's take a look at the different picture—missing the party because you genuinely believe, with every fiber of your being, that you are only an introvert. If you're stuck in the middle of the two, I will say, it's not allowing yourself to do what you enjoy because of your situation. This should never happen. That's one takeaway with this chapter: Stick to what you like and have your fun! Don't take on an unhappy life out of hesitancy to interact with others.

In my situation, I shared with you how I love to express myself with dancing. I love to dance. Well, in my freshman year of college, I missed some parties, if not most of them. I'm so serious. I finally tried "the spot" that everyone had been dancing in for the last month of school. By then, the excitement was gone because my friends had been coming all year without me. Talk about a bummer of a school year, and to think that it was my first freshman year; the thought still makes me cringe today.

I was so bogged down with intensive reading (studying) that I refused to have much fun. I had convinced myself that I would enjoy studying tonight, instead, because I had liked staying in the house. I was probably regressing from the headache of having to keep up with friends and their conversations in a club. I knew the club scene would be loud and that people would be trying to party, instead of having to repeat things for me. It took me a long time to create my own happiness while in a club and have fun while everyone else communicated and had fun. My final decision was to simply dance and enjoy the music, and in my view, there was nothing wrong with that.

When we overthink, a disability can become overwhelming.

The truth is, the hearing loss is going to be there regardless, but never let it stop you from doing those things that make you happy. Never allow it to overwhelm and use up much valuable time when you could be enjoying yourself. This is a habit, if taken too lightly, that can lead to severe depression. This depression would come as the result of regret for not deciding to be stronger, taking the chance to enjoy life, and to do what makes you happy.

Face the Struggle

Living in a state of hesitation and refusing to face the struggle, we sometimes convince ourselves that we would rather stay home, but what we're really doing is avoiding interaction. Let's face it, some people speak extremely low, and it's annoying. It's so nerve-racking to be in a group of people, and then a low-toned person takes over the conversation. "Really, do you actually expect me to hear you talking that low?"

Things happen that cause us to regress and sometimes decline invitations. When this cycle continues, we find ourselves unhappy because we are no longer able to fully enjoy our lives. The answer to this is figuring out whether you are truly an introvert or extrovert and working from there. Why should you take the time to figure this out? First, self-identification is incredible, and second, it will assure you that you never allow your situation to make you unhappy or regretful.

> *If you are, in fact, an introvert, that doesn't excuse you from the "hesitancy to socialize" factor.*

Many people who are introverts prefer not to socialize. However, socializing is an integral part of life. Socializing allows you to learn your culture, your surroundings, and your identity—your preferred lifestyle. It might even be the driving factor to help you understand your ultimate role in life or what is expected of you by others.

Have you ever taken a self-assessment test? I have completed a few, and I find them very interesting, no matter how funny, wrong, or shocking they may be. One of the main questions always asked is, "What do people come to you for?" Hmmm, how will you know this if you never socialize? How will you know what you can contribute if you never socialize with others? My point exactly… you won't. I can't reiterate enough the number of times I was in regressive phases of my life, and unable to understand my gift to the world. My contribution to society came to me when I was at peace in my life and open to socializing and mingling with others.

Consider a social media fast...

Therefore, until you have figured out your life's destiny, consider limiting social media time or challenge yourself to a social media fast. This is serious business, I might add. Why a social media cutback when social media is socializing? Well, first, because it's reckless socializing and let's face it, what can you do with five thousand friends, when you can barely understand your own likes and dislikes? How happy can you be for others when nothing new is happening in your life? Are you truly happy listening to others brag and gloat while your life is mediocre? To each his own, is what I will say.

Truthfully, this advice may not be for everyone. You may have done a social media fast in the past six months and don't feel the need to. If so, then great job and more power to you. If not, however, let's examine one of the obvious negative dynamics of social media on the lesser hearing; it includes countless self-made videos that usually don't include closed captioning. Could this be any worse? This could be the first ticker that frustrates you when you don't know your priorities. This silly video that adds no value to your life gets to frustrate the crap out of you, but yet, it adds nothing to your well-being. It's about knowing priorities. Yes, your priorities. What will be your contribution to the world? What is your talent, and how are you using it to further the lesser hearing community or even your local community?

> *Social media is a huge distraction that can cut life dreams and aspirations back by eighty miles per hour.*

Social media is very detrimental to those who have not invested time in understanding their personal legacy. We see so many glamorous photos and ads of vacations, expensive restaurants, my new book, my new business, my new baby, my trip to Spain, and the storylines (the posts) that never end. Answer this question: Would you really stop and give your time to each person on your page, if they walked past you on the street? I doubt that you would, so why should you give that precious time away now, just because the location has changed, and you are sitting in front of a computer? Wasted time is just that—no matter where it happens.

Aside from wasted time, my point is that there is a tendency for social media to be so darn distracting that by merely taking our first step to think about our talents and gifts is a mountain to climb. How much time can you donate to thinking about your future after reading fifty posts of different opinions, remarks, occasions, news updates, ads, and so forth? How focused can you be on setting quarterly and annual goals for yourself? Do you get my drift? Do you need a social media fast? I think you do. Personally, I fast from social media every quarter for thirty days. I have even fasted for up to six months. Those have been most replenishing, and I really didn't miss much because everyone that needed to contact me could simply call or shoot me an email.

Avoid Becoming an Outcast

Getting better with socializing will also help you to avoid becoming an outcast. Whether you're fifteen, twenty-one, thirty-one, forty-five, or seventy, it's never good to be an outcast. This is what you will become when you continue to decline outings and miss events. People will get tired of your rejections and stop inviting you. Of course, I experienced that, too. I wouldn't write it if I didn't know it to be true. As an author, I always want to share my stories so that others don't take themselves through the same devastating experiences. The law of attraction is real, and what you put out there, you will get back. Place rejection out there, and you will get rejection back. Place acceptance out there, and you will get acceptance back.

Just as I declined to go with the crew to parties in my freshman year of college, they soon stopped asking me to come. It was just that simple. This crew of girls was exceptionally kind and friendly, so I now know that when they stopped inviting me, it was me. Yet, I was stuck in a dorm room, obsessing over my hearing, and missing a wonderful chance to get out and enjoy life! I became an outcast, and by the end of the year, I had to ask them to please remind me when they went again so that I wouldn't miss it for the world. Up until then, I could feel them regressing from me as I had regressed from them earlier. I wasn't aware before of what they expected of me because I wasn't socializing. As I said earlier, socializing is about understanding what's expected of you.

> *When we learn most about ourselves,*
> *it is through human interaction.*

As a human, you have your right to days and times of withdrawal. Just be sure not to make a habit of avoiding socializing. Whether it's in small groups or large groups doesn't matter.

What we have to realize is that we learn about ourselves mostly through human interaction. Being introverted all of the time is a refusal to break out of your comfort zone; your comfort zone will never help you to be successful. Take it a step further and learn how to adjust to these events for your own good. This goes a long way as you move forward in life and learn to socialize better. This is what well-rounded people do; that is what you are aiming to become. That is what will place you at your best anywhere—the ability to socialize. What you choose for your life is all within your power. You could desire to visit snow-capped mountains, warm sandy beaches, or walks in the rain; however, if you won't even leave the house to experience them, well then, what is the point?

*A hearing disability doesn't alter
your ability to socialize… you do.*

After all is said and done, you will love yourself for it. Here's a thought: It's the good times that you will remember. That's the truth. How many times have you tripped in a large group of people, or walked out of the restroom with toilet paper on your shoes while at a nice event? You probably barely remember. And that's because when we're genuinely having a good time, those memories will automatically take precedence over any mishaps. It's the way of the world, and you have to trust it. But first, you have to get out there and keep socializing.

This chapter gave a push in the right direction for socializing; next, I will share how to better relate in the workplace!

CHAPTER 5

Bring You're "A" Game... Change How You Relate in Your Workplace!

> *"Each time we face our fear, we gain strength, courage, and confidence in the doing."*
> —Theodore Roosevelt
> *Physically Challenged Former POTUS*

WHY THEODORE ROOSEVELT POPPED into my mind at the beginning of this chapter, I am not sure, but through his astounding accomplishments, I cannot beg to differ that he is the perfect person to begin this chapter with. He truly made his workplace work for him, which enabled him, even as President of the United States, to always be at his best! That is what I want to help you to do in this chapter. Did you know that, before he moved into the White House, ramps were added to make it more wheelchair friendly? Talk about power, confidence, and high esteem.

But first, I want to share my own experience of leveling up in my career. As a real estate professional in Washington, D.C., I found myself engrossed in one of the world's most competitive and prestigious professions! I was on my "A" game and wore it to work every single day! I negotiated contracts, set offer prices, partnered with co-op agents, and power networked in one of the most competitive locations of the world. There was never a dull day. Clients wanted everything (they were paying top dollar), and investors wanted max profits. However, at the end of the day, my empathy was with my clients. I'm sort of a nurturer, and the experiences of my clients are what matter most to me. But there is always a catch to life, right?

Here's the catch

You may not yet be aware of this, but people are surprisingly more patient with you (and your impairment) when there is a guaranteed benefit for them. Maybe this is something that the people who elected Roosevelt knew they would receive. First, I will say this: my clients always accepted that I was hearing impaired upfront. There was no hiding it, or hesitancy to introduce it as a part of myself because it simply was part of me. I like to think that I set this tone during consultations when I introduced myself with confidence, hearing aid, and all. I would gladly answer their questions about it, but I didn't make it an issue either. I believe that what you make an issue, others will make an issue. If they did ask questions, I answered them promptly and assured them that I was a diligent worker with excellent capabilities. I then explained to them the concept of "their home, their choice."

This approach simply meant that clients would not be pressured into purchasing or selling anything, that they would continually be educated about everything, and that my door was always open for questions, or moments of reassurance. After all, buying a home is your most substantial investment, right?

I didn't notice this fondness that my clients had for me until I was nearly ten years in. I began to see how much loyalty overrides any type of impairment. I mean, it was truly amazing. My clients would text me important questions if we had low phone connections or send a long email with all of their concerns to suit my preference in communications methods. As long as I read the entire email and handled their issues, why should they care about the mode of communication?

I mean, no, they were not "eating out of my hand," but they were pretty graceful when working with me. They were accommodating for me because they wanted to work with me. They trusted and valued my professionalism and word of mouth referral goes a long way in an area like Washington, D.C. After ten years in the real estate game, I started to receive more referrals and repeat business than ever before. This was a major uplift to my spirit because our hearing loss can sometimes cause us to question whether it has blocked us from being the best that we can be. In this case, it was clear that it had not.

For you to tackle what I am saying, I will say it again: *People are patient when there is a guaranteed benefit for them.* Everyone around the table has more tolerance and fortitude when you have shown them your worth, and that my dear, is the big idea behind this chapter. Do you know your professional worth? Do you exhibit and claim your professional value? Or do you simply sit behind a desk and do as you are told, waiting for others' acknowledgment? Just like when Cuba Gooding's character encouraged his agent, played by Tom Cruise, to holler into the phone, "Show me the money," in the movie *Jerry Maguire*. He was indirectly saying, "I know my worth, so go tell them my worth." Well, in this chapter, I'm telling you to *show them your worth.*

Everyone around the table simply has more tolerance and fortitude when you have shown them your worth.

When we think of the word *show*, most people immediately equate it to the concept of "showing off." My positive state of mind enables me to see the word "show" as "proof." So, in other words, prove to them your worth. Prove to them that you're capable; it will go a step further than saying it, and if you follow through with it, it's a powerful and promising approach. It's my opinion that living with such a situation tends to spark this keen desire to "show people" or "give them proof." It sparks a desire to be valued, so use it.

Work Hard or Not at All

I was hardworking, and yet I didn't want to over-promise what I could not deliver. Working hard would mean that they would work with me along the way because they had seen my efforts. I had the chance to get my feet wet, but I also had to "show" them that I was always working on it, or still on top of the deal.

However, there were challenges since my area was such a competitive field. I didn't want to over-promise a detached two-car garage with the perfect location when your money limited you to a townhouse with community parking in a "not so great" neighborhood. And so, being the facilitator that I am, I wanted to show people that I would always be working hard for them. When they see me working hard for them and making every effort, if there ever came a time that they had to forego a feature in a home, then they weren't as insistent because they had seen my hard work.

Does that make sense? It's the psychology behind people seeing and understanding that you are diligent and disciplined; they feel like they can depend on you and are able to overlook the hearing device.

> *Without understanding your skillset, you will not understand what you could "show off" or complete as if it's "second nature."*

Know and understand your skillset...

That brings me to my next point… know and understand your skillset. Without this, you won't recognize what you could "show off" or complete as if it's "second nature." My skillset was people skills and bonding, listening skills, and teaching. Of course, using a strategy such as this also requires superb communication, bonding with clients, and mutual trust. More than anything, I think it was a matter of understanding my skillset. I knew that I was good at winning the sympathy of others by working hard. I knew that I was great at listening and bonding with clients. I knew that I was great at creating mutual trust and never risking client trust. So, I had defined my skillset as great communication, bonding, teaching, and mutual trust.

Here's an example: Let's say that the sellers didn't choose the best contractor for your buyer's repairs and the seller may have to complete thirty plus repairs, but they have no money whatsoever. Well, what do you do in situations such as this? You simply show up and try. You bond with them and sympathize with them. You show them that you will work hard to get them what they want—so that whatever the outcome, they appreciate your professionalism and efforts.

In no way am I assuming that you are not making enough efforts in your work life; this may very well be a well-accomplished attribute of yourself, and if it is, then BRAVO! However, for those of us that sulk and sigh through the workday, CUT IT OUT! Let's first agree that I am not the only one here interacting every day in my workplace with a hearing loss.

Let's consider a mutual agreement between us, that we simply cannot expect people in our work world to always be perfectly patient with our situation. Nope, not always going to happen. We have to give them a reason to be patient, and the proof that we deserve it will be shown in our actions. If you are looking for that perfect client, perfect boss, or perfect professor, then I'm just going to be real with you and say, NO WAY JOSE! There is just not that much love floating around here on planet earth, and the reality is that we don't have the luxury of choosing our work world contacts, like we can choose our friends and companions.

Nope, the purpose behind these relationships is different. Different in a good way, because this is a workplace, and if you conquer your plans, make your sale, attain your promotion, or earn your certification, this will help them see your value.

People don't mean to be mean.

Don't get me wrong; people don't intend to be mean. They really don't. They are simply overwhelmed with the day, never taking a break, never rejuvenating, working mediocre jobs that bring no happiness, and staying married to people who aren't making them happy, just because they think it's great for the kids! Whew! Did I get it all in there? Anything sound familiar? This is simply the day and age that we live in.

People don't make space for you on a park bench; they pull up and steal your parking space, or drive up to the rear of your car, shining headlights just to get you to speed up! Oh, my God... I'm laughing at myself again. I swear, I love writing. However, my point is that if they won't make an effort to keep themselves in check and avoid flying off the handle, why would they make that effort for you and your feelings? Hey, it's nothing personal. This just hits close to home with me, because for years, I waited for the world to "grow a little nicer," or for people to "speak a little louder"—without me suggesting it.

Focus on what you can change. . . and that is you.

We have to realize that none of their behaviors have anything to do with us! The cashier with the attitude is upset because she has to walk home after being on her feet for five hours. The Uber driver didn't greet you when he picked you up because this job is barely making ends meet, and Christmas is right around the corner. Or, the co-worker never speaks to you because she is an introvert. None of these people, or their situations, have anything to do with you. With that being said, you can now stop focusing your energies on them and focus on yourself. Focus on what you can change, and that is you. Focus on knowing your skillset and using it to prove yourself.

In order to always "be at your best," there will always be a need to consistently prove yourself, especially in your work life. Come on, break out of your shell, and throw a suggestion out there at the next staff meeting, step up to your supervisor, ask for more responsibilities, or be a reliable worker who's always fifteen minutes early for work. Like I tend to say to people a lot, "I dare you." My point is not to look for people to be patient with your situation if they have nothing to gain. It's not common or typical.

People (especially in business) are patient with us when we partner with them in circumstances where they benefit. If you're an average employee, and your superiors feel that they are simply covering you (by employing you), you absolutely have to show them your worth; that shall pass many others that they cover (employ)! Make them proud that they hired you. Learn names and become motivated in the workplace. Smile and greet people. Give people a firm handshake and smile often. This is your first step to power networking, starting with yourself. It's time to make you an asset.

Assets vs. Liabilities

Assets are partners who bring value to a company. Liabilities are workers who bring risks to a company. Did you catch what I just said? Okay, so question… which are you? I've had quite enough work experience, playing both roles in my life to know when I am an asset to an employer and when I am a liability. In both work environments, colleague's treatment of you, the patience they have with you, and their enthusiasm to work with you, should show you, clearly, whether you're an asset or a liability.

Here's an example: Two thousand sixteen had been a hectic year for me in real estate. I had closed a good amount of home sales, and I was ready to kick up my heels and close the year out with my family, celebrating Christmas. My clients were set to settle in their new home in the third week of December, right before Christmas. The inspections and appraisals had been completed, and all loan documents had been signed. This had been a nine-month Short Sale deal that began in March, and we were finally closing now in December. The only thing left to complete was a pre-settlement walkthrough, and we would be home free. My clients and I pulled up to the house two days before settlement, unlocked the front door, and went inside.

The home looked beautiful, it even smelled beautiful, but something was wrong. It was freezing! Apparently, the previous seller had already called the utility company to shut off the water and electricity. This meant that my buyers wouldn't be able to test out the heat; they were frantic, and of course, I empathized with them. I calmly relayed to them that I would never ask them to forfeit a pre-settlement walkthrough, and I reminded them that this is what they hired me for and that I would get them into their warm home before Christmas.

Over the next few hours, I worked anxiously with the cooperating agent to track down the seller, so the electric could be connected to complete the walkthrough and close on time, and that we did, not a second later! My clients wrote great online reviews for my quick and efficient services, and once again, I made myself an asset to my company by proving myself. I had branded myself as a company asset.

Now, on the liability side, a few years earlier, in 2010, after I had given birth to my daughter, I decided to respite from the real estate life and work as a teacher assistant for a while. I was assigned to assist a kindergarten teacher who had just come back from maternity leave. We both arrived in the classroom on the same day. She was frantic because she was not ready to return to work after having her second child and felt that the previous substitute teacher had destroyed her class. She was aware of my impairment, as it had been explained to her by our employer, not myself (big mistake).

After a few weeks of feeling as if she had to continually observe me, she began to refuse to talk to me directly and simply passed me a note (on a sticky) when she needed something. She refused to let me actively teach the lesson plan out of fear that I would "mess up something." I mean, come on. . . it was kindergarten. What was I going to mess up, singing nursery rhymes? It was discouraging, and I was bewildered. It was the perfect case of myself refusing to jump in there, figure out my skillset, and sell myself. What was I doing? I was sulking and sighing. I was questioning myself. I was becoming a company liability.

It was a discriminatory situation and seemed to be one of the longest teaching positions that I had ever completed because sometimes, co-workers who cannot adapt bring severe stress. She had begun to see me as a risk to her and her teaching environment, and I felt the bite of this. The assistant principal was monitoring teacher performances one day and was very upset with the approach that this teacher had taken for communicating with me. "How will the students open up and accept Ms. Briscoe if you won't?" She asked. This teacher didn't budge; she didn't care. Nevertheless, I continued to do the best that I could.

A few weeks later, we held a mediation hearing, initiated by the assistant principal; the teacher was given a warning and told to halt what had been documented as rude and discriminatory behavior toward me. She was warned that she was expected to be more proactive with me and more respectful to me. I had officially become a government liability, and the feeling was gruesome. There are not enough meetings and write-ups in the world that can null the pain of discrimination. I still remember moments of this time in my life, today, like it was yesterday. I remember sitting at a round table, surrounded by officials and afraid to speak up about what I needed as an employee, or what I offered as an employee. Honestly, I was in a withdrawal phase in my life, and I didn't want them to help me. Better yet, I began to feel that everyone was simply pondering how to best save the company from a discriminatory lawsuit. Where was their regard for me, and what would be most suitable?

In order for people to understand your needs, you will have to tell them.

Disability discrimination is real, alive, and kicking. However, it can only have the power that we give it. In order for people to understand your needs, you will have to tell them. Stop making an issue about the fact that you have to reveal what accommodations you need to let people into your lives. Maybe it's worth being a little vulnerable to fulfill this internal desire to get just as much of a fair chance as the next person.

If you're uncomfortable answering phones, then say it. Ask them if accommodations can be made. If it's a company that's not financially able to accommodate your needs, then nicely ask them to consider removing this responsibility from your job description. Whatever you do, don't sit there distraught while answering phones, barely hearing callers, and taking yourself through that roller coaster of emotions.

The Roller Coaster of Emotions

Let's just put it out there. When we run into tasks that we have to complete at work, we want to be just as good as (or hopefully better) than the next person. We want to be given our responsibilities and to be able to master them successfully, just as well as others. This is pretty human, and there is nothing wrong with this at all. The roller coaster of emotions comes at times when we refuse to speak up about those tasks that are just too much for us.

We receive our daily work log. We review the list of everything that we can knock out of the park with no problem (like emails, texts, and writing a memo). But then we give a try to the old telephone calls and uhhh… here comes the roller coaster of emotions. Here come the upset callers who have no idea that you will struggle to hear everything that they say. What brought my roller coaster of emotions was not a telephone. It was the children that I taught who talked extra soft and low. Oh, my goodness, I dreaded certain hours of the day, the hours where I had to tend to their needs and stretch and struggle to hear what they were saying, hanging on to their every word.

This time of the day brought sadness and discouragement. I was happy when the time for constant interaction and communication with them ended (like nap time). I could relax during these times, but I did not realize that I shouldn't have to work like this every day, struggling and straining. And neither should you. In fact, there are but so many emotions that you should feel about a job every day. Don't get me wrong—positive emotions are always great. Yet, when we talk about negative emotions and handling them, we need to understand that, when we have to repeatedly overcome these dreaded tasks, they do affect our ability to do the job and do it with the best attitude. Therefore, assignments that negatively test your emotions should be limited.

I mean, these emotions can pretty much tear your day apart. I'm talking about positions, such as online customer service reps, when you know your struggle is all day long every day. How motivated could you be clocking into a job like that every single day? And sensibly, why would we do that to ourselves? Maybe you like your current position and are willing to work with some things in your current role. But if you're not strong enough to speak up for accommodating yourself and eliminating specific responsibilities to avoid the emotion draining, then maybe it's not the job for you.

Who can I blame if I never speak up for myself? Where would I even begin to cover myself with an unhappy caller client, if my boss doesn't know that I cannot hear on the phone? I know that earlier I said that people are mean, and I stand by that. However, in the work world, employers and supervisors don't have the luxury of "acting how they want to." Tell a supervisor that you need to be texted regarding your shift instead of calling you. If he doesn't accommodate you, then he is in for it. His supervisor won't like it, and neither will their superiors. We live in a country where CEOs, federal and local government agencies, and all other organizations, firms, and work environments have pledged to honor you and your needs as a hired worker.

The Entrepreneurship Throne

I shared these two instances because I wanted to detail my experience in two different work environments—corporate commissioned-based and governmental settings. One is an environment where the ball is in your court, and you call the shots; the other is a "take what we give you" arena. Which one would you prefer?

Entrepreneurship has allowed me to cut to the chase, push myself, and see what a great worker I am. I didn't have to be assigned to assist ignorant co-workers who couldn't handle their emotions. I didn't have to be subjected to demoting situations that would not allow me to excel and begin to feel great about myself as a teacher. On the flip side, entrepreneurship allowed me to recognize that people really do see past impairments, allowing you to service them, if you are sure to do a great job. In business, we congratulate each other on sales and listings, while teachers and government co-workers simply looked forward to holiday breaks.

> *Be sure that you have a work environment that offers you the freedom to excel and to be at your best.*

Working as a government employee meant much more interaction with co-workers and sometimes having to be among a few negative people who were unhappy with themselves, just trying to make a check. It was an exhausting experience, and I now realize that the only reason I returned was for financial stability after the birth of my daughter. After I received that stability and was back on my feet, I jetted back to my real estate office and colleagues. The flexibility in hours was awesome, and I also branded and marketed myself, which soared my confidence as well.

Whew, Chile! Talk about two very different environments. I feel as if God took me through this walk to share this, when it comes to working confidently with a hearing loss. My point is, be sure you have a work environment that offers you the freedom to excel and be at your best. That means working among others who see you as an asset, not a liability.

Entrepreneurship is always great, but it's not the perfect fit for everyone, and that's fine. Just be sure that where you choose to work, you exhibit and demonstrate your skillset, so those you serve have a chance to receive you as an asset and not a liability.

It may sound as if I am a bit hostile to the traditional non-entrepreneurship roles. But that's not the case. My gesture is that you simply understand and give a chance to be your own leader, because no one is going to understand your needs more than you. Your clients will return to you continually with bonding and mutual trust. It was a win-win for me, and it could be for you as well. Just never feel like you have to "settle" for what you can get because of a hearing impairment. That attitude will land you in the wrong position every time.

Do your research...

Some governmental agencies and private sector companies do pretty well, providing accommodations to their employees. In order to recognize these companies, we must do our research first. I know that job searches are hard enough, but this is an additional and critical step that we have to take for ourselves. "The good news is that there are a lot of companies that have exceptional work environments that make it a priority to recruit disabled employees." As I dove deeper into my job searches, I also dove deeper into company research, to be sure that "my" company supported me. I found a few companies to offer extraordinary things.

These companies may not be located in your area, but it will give you a dose of enthusiasm in your job searches. Just as we don't settle in personal relationships, we should not settle in work relationships. KPMG has a Disability Network within its company and takes great pride in retaining feedback from its workers. Diversity Inc. even named KPMG (an

International Cooperative) as one of the TOP fifty companies for diversity.

S.C. Johnson supports and advocates for its employees who deal with a loss. This is awesome; it's almost as if their employees have someone in their corner to speak up for them, instead of just "meeting needs." I couldn't think of a better way to welcome these employees. S.C. Johnson is also known for its great recruiting program that hires and trains hearing loss employees.

> *Companies that are more fluent in expending these accommodations tend to provide more comfortable work environments.*

What can you get from working with a company that already has these resources in place? You will get an environment that is easier for you to share your concerns. You will get staff awareness, meaning co-workers will respect you as part of the company culture. You will get assurance that the company has dealt with disability issues and that you will not be the first to voice your concerns. Those are three excellent reasons to look eagerly for companies that already have their accommodations and awareness programs in place.

One of the next suggestions that I would give to you would be to check out websites, programs, and connections that already have your impairment in mind and go from there. One such resource is EARN (Employer Assistance and Resource Network on Disability Inclusion). This program helps employers to build an inclusive culture within the workplace. It's a helpful resource to use if you have developed a great relationship with your superiors. It could be used as a self-explanatory resource to help them better understand disability inclusion. This resource itself is a great one in my eyes, and it's used throughout the U.S.

On the website, you can look at their job seeker resources tab and get started with a job search that gives you favor because of your hearing loss! See Resources IV on the Resources page for the website. It's so important, when we apply for jobs, that we step into acceptable environments. In that aspect, I mean, do your research and apply through organizations and websites that give preference for disabled. Set up your next job (or career step) within a company that wants you there and has already invested in ways to accommodate you before you were employed with them.

The story that I described earlier, working in the school system, is a perfect example of a workplace that was not prepared to accommodate me. Try your best to avoid these types of workplaces. You don't want to be their "chance to test out their strategies that help avoid lawsuits" because they never thought to accommodate their workers until you showed up with your demands. Being this intuitive beforehand, and doing the research is not an approach that many of us take, but believe me, it's a big deal. If it's not handled now, then it will become an issue later, that is a given.

Finally, you absolutely must retain a Schedule "A" letter. The Schedule "A" letter is written by a licensed professional that can attest to the severity of your impairment and agree that you should be hired under the Schedule "A" hiring authority within the Federal Government. Please consider taking a trip to your licensed physician for this supportive letter that will place you ahead of a lot of competition. After I received mine and told friends and family, I received so many responses with wishes that they could use such a letter.

They know, like you and I both know, that job searches can be difficult. This is something that I have heard has gotten many people in the door for Federal Government positions. And if your searches have been long and drawn out, then it's definitely worth giving it a try. Schedule "A" letters are used exclusively in the Federal Government during its hiring process. The law requires that the Federal Government make reasonable accommodations to those who are qualified. What does this mean? This means that if you are eligible for the position, the Federal Government must make the accommodation for you to work that position. The Federal Government may offer interpreters, modify your position duties, provide flexible work schedules or work sites. They may even take it a step further and provide accessible technology for you. It's all in your hands, and it's totally your call.

Adjusting to Your Environment

In Chapter 4, I lightly touched on the value of knowing what work environments you can flourish in. However, it goes much further than that. Which tone of voice can you hear? Which settings are calm enough and which are too distracting? Which clients articulate well, and which barely part their lips (which I cannot stand)? Which clients love the email chain (which I find very beneficial) and simply refuse to check their emails?

> *You must communicate what accommodations you will need to best adjust to your environment and breed success in your work life.*

All of these attributes will affect how well you are able to perform your job; it is worth figuring out sooner, rather than later. According to the National Research Council (U.S.) Committee on Disability Determination for Individuals with Hearing Impairments, "When hearing loss occurs during adulthood, [even] after completion of formal education and after the establishment of a work history or career, it poses challenges for job performances and future job mobility. Because these adults have already acquired the knowledge and skills needed to perform their jobs, the difficulties they face are related to communication barriers, such as working conditions and employer attitudes."

So, as this section emphasizes, you must communicate what accommodations you will need to best adjust to your environment, in order to breed success in your work life.

Although the article targets those who have experienced the loss as adults, the fact remains that hearing loss does pose challenges for job performance, regardless of when you acquired the loss.

Let me share with you something that happened to me amid my teaching career. After college, I worked as a Special Education high school teacher. The hallways were always loud, with kids shouting excitedly at 9 a.m. Because of my hearing loss, this was not bothersome to me at all. In fact, it was the perfect work environment for me; I loved my students. They never had to be asked to repeat themselves because they naturally talked loudly and full of enthusiasm.

They appreciated being able to complete classwork with excitement during class. As I think back, the way I ran my class was a little amusing because I never really said "quiet down" much. My students and I bonded as I taught them and shared coping strategies with them. Although some minimal adjustments needed to be made, my work environment was comfortable.

Teenagers don't pass judgment a lot; they are in a time when they are deciding who they are, and they don't knock anyone for being the way that they are. They made me feel very accepted as their teacher. I had an exceptional assistant, Emily, who worked wonders for me. She was patient with both the children and me; she was charming and so full of grace. She was simply one of those people who worked well with those faced with disabilities.

I did not know that, years later, I would give early childhood education a try, a job that required working with very young kids between the ages of three and five. Silly me, is what I will say now, after the entire "ordeal" was over. It was awful. I loved the little Pre-K toddlers, but I just couldn't hear them... uhhh. They always wanted more snacks or a bathroom break, but due to their young age, they had such undeveloped speech articulation skills. They commented low in the reading circle, and over time, I found that it was just not conducive to my teaching abilities. I could barely use my teaching abilities. I was so stressed and unhappy. My work environment was requiring adjustments that I just could not make. It just didn't seem possible to continue.

My principal didn't consider my concerns and refused to allow me to work with older kids. She was pregnant at the time and very frustrated and cranky. As the previous paragraph suggested, "employer attitudes" can have an impact, which was definitely the case. When she took her leave of absence to give birth, the interim principal walked throughout the school on his first day on the job. He called me at home that evening and arranged for a meeting in his office the next day. He spoke to me about my needs. He asked me what he could do to help me to correctly assist the children. That day, he requested that I be moved to a kindergarten class with the older, louder, and more mature group. They were a little better with word articulation, as well. I was relieved. The adjustments that I made were realistic, and it worked for the end of the school term, but still to this day, it would not be the age group that I prefer, simply because their articulation skills are not matured enough for my level of hearing either.

It worked out well as I ended the school year, but afterward, I vowed that this would be my final year teaching young children. It was so very tiring and stressful to try and hear what I just could not hear (toddler voices). It was a time in my life when I realized that the stress of repeating was too much for the children to bear, and the stress of asking them to repeat themselves was too much for me to bear.

Workplace discrimination is real, and you must always analyze your work environment and the population that you are serving.

I was grateful for the temporary placement, but I didn't need anyone to "save me," as this interim principal did. I had already made this suggestion myself to the original principal and was not heard. It took a toll on my views of employee discrimination, and I was upset that I had to experience workplace discrimination once again. It was very much an eye-opener experience for me, and it was the year I saw myself as a liability in my workplace. What if a child was hurt (thank God that never happened)? What if there was no one around who could correctly interpret what a child was asking for?

That was a year that all sorts of insecurities ran through my mind. But the biggest insecurity was seeing myself as a liability and not an asset, as I had been in my real estate business. Why should work be this hard, just because I harbor a hearing loss?

I decided that teaching young children had to end. I needed better articulation with every fiber of my being. Thankfully, it would work out for the better as I decided to seek out a career that would grant more leadership opportunities.

I still mentor high school and young adults to this day, because they can speak and articulate well. They have a nature that is always interesting and curious to me. If you ever want a nonjudgmental chill group to relax with, then there you have it! Why am I speaking about this? Because it's an angle that we never investigate. We never do the work of ensuring that the positions we pursue will not be too challenging for us and that accommodations will be made. We simply apply for jobs and struggle to work them, but we don't realize that we risk ourselves, and our employers feel as though we are risking them. At least, this was my experience. As I said before, workplace discrimination is real, and you must always analyze your work environment and the population that you are serving.

The truth is, you will never be able to excel in a position if the position works against your needs. It's just not possible. This is why you must find employers that accommodate your disability or allow you flexibility in your workplace, where you can see how you could be successful. This story is one of many that I have, and I know that I am one of the millions with an account of such. I know that you have a few stories up your sleeves, as well.

The good news is that there are many positions where it is possible to excel. Many jobs don't require us to answer phones or talk with low responding recipients. Even being a presenter from time to time can become complicated, but I learned to prepare myself for it with my devices and meditation. I train my ears, mind, and heart to receive as much as I can because writing is a passion, and I don't have an employer standing over me, micromanaging my every step. The floor is mine. It's another great gift that I receive when I perform special events and encourage others, sharing the message for inspiration.

Since we have discussed how to receive accommodations in the workplace, I figure now would be the time to talk about gearing up and coming prepared with a hearing device suitable for you. What I recommend are traditional hearing aid devices that are Bluetooth compatible with the workplace. In Chapter 2, I talked about the remarkable features of the device, but I also shared the importance of knowing your hearing severity levels. All of this knowledge comprises to help you become a better, more aware employee, which will allow you to become an asset to your company.

Regardless, we are in a day and age that you don't have to go to work bare. I have had a few friends disclose that they never took the time to learn how to work the Bluetooth device on their hearing aid. This is completely ludicrous. Think of how much ease a Bluetooth connected to a hearing aid gives you and then tell me again, why you would not partake in this magnificent creation. So, who is really in the wrong here?

When people see a hearing aid, they think one of two things: (1) That you have a hearing aid, so you can simply adjust and work just as well as the next person. Or (2) they think that they will have to continually guide and assist you.

Both approaches are absurd, but now the question becomes, who is in the wrong here? The employer or the employee? People don't know that wearing a hearing aid will not give you perfect hearing, just as they are not aware of the benefits of hearing devices that don't require you to be assisted by anyone. Let me let you in on a little secret that I have figured out over time. . .some people want to help you be a better worker. You just have to tell them how you work and adjust to your environment.

In the case that you decide now to disclose, are you wrong for refusing to communicate your needs to superiors upfront? Are you always transparent about your needs with a new employer, or do you try to avoid "rocking the boat" as a new face in a company? I will say that I have been the latter and don't claim that with pride at all. Yes, not rocking the boat is an easier approach, but it's also a stressful one. And why should everyone else live a stress-free life while you twist and struggle because you don't want them to know the truth?

I am beyond guilty of this, and this is one of the reasons that I have always drawn back to my real estate business. As I expressed before, my buyers always come to me referred and preferring my services. So, yes, of course, it's easy to tell them what I will need from them. It's easy to suggest that they check their listings that I send every morning at 8:00 a.m. because this is how I work, and they respect that. It's not so easy in many governmental or private-sector jobs. My point is that you have to convey your needs, or you will stress. You have to be aware of your needs, or you will struggle.

Is the employer wrong for not catering every position to suit your needs with accommodations? Are there positions that an employer should be able to refuse to hire you for? For example, following high school, I wanted to go into the military branch, but living in my father's house and hearing his mouth just about discouraged me. I appreciated the military's discipline and all that they had to offer; however, I was internally discouraged by my hearing loss when I should not have been. If anything, it would have been the perfect job to attain excellent benefits for exams, hearing aids, and even cochlear implant surgery.

I have discovered that most employers have been required to do as much as they can to address the workplace needs over the years. However, it is up to us to know the skills and qualifications that we bring. Furthermore, it is up to us to have internally examined what work environments have made us uncomfortable and try to refrain from those places. I didn't say that I would never be a teacher again; I said I would not teach below kindergarten grade-level and preferred working with the older students.

Ask for what you need. Employers aren't mind readers.

Here's a thought: In my own experience, within the places that I have worked, there was a tendency for employers to be at a loss on how to suit my needs and fifty percent of the time, it was not because they were neglectful, but simply because I didn't ask for what I needed. I feel like this is more common than some people care to admit. When I attended mediation with my principal while working with a teacher who refused to communicate respectfully with me, the principal had to practically beg me to elaborate on my needs and what was happening in the classroom, making me uncomfortable.

There is no exaggeration in this statement. Her words were, "Ms. Briscoe. We want to know what you need this teacher to do. How can we help to make you more productive here?"

The truth is, I was so afraid that by disclosing this to a full staff, it would be received as a hindrance to my ability to do my job. This fear and hesitancy should not have been happening within me. This fear cannot happen if our community wants to move forward and gain our place in society. I should have used this time in my workplace to move beyond the shadow of a doubt that my hearing loss had brought upon me.

The battlefield of equality...

Our workplace is not the place to draw a blank when it comes to how we can best do our jobs. It's the place to defeat the enemy. It is the battlefield for which our equality can take its first step. I know that this is happening among people because it happened to me, a hearing advocate. We all have our stories, but if this is your current story, I urge you to let the truth be brought to life and have faith that God will not leave you with a burden that He entrusted you with.

So, what if that employer chose to fire me? Maybe I would have gotten to my dream job then. Yet, I had not chosen to stay in a workplace that didn't honor me as the worker that I was. Still, what matters most is that we try; try in our work, try in our home lives, and try in our every day. When we do this, we can live with whatever situations prevail, but at least we know that we tried.

H.R. departments should be very well-trained to work with you. Taking time to disclose allows them to begin to ask their questions. They may ask if you prefer 1:1 meetings or how your hearing may affect what you are assigned to do at work. Healthy workplaces will reassure you that they will help you to manage your hearing loss at work. Some may even offer to have your hearing checked, which should not be taken as a threat that they may fire you or demote you; there are many laws against this. The purpose of the check is to help them comprehend the severity of your hearing loss with much more supportive information than you can offer them.

To disclose or not to disclose...

There is a way to escape the "dreadful" conversations of disclosing and simply prepare a written statement. I recommend this because it allows employers an opportunity to read and process the entire document without fear, panic, or quick countering questions. As I grew in my career, I began to use this type of disclosure when employed because it seemed to "clear the air." After an employer receives this, they will usually meet with you, a little more aware and responsive to your needs. Many people respect and appreciate what is written on paper.

I was reading an excellent article last week, posted by the New York Times. It detailed how to disclose a disability to your employer. In the article, it spoke of a legal director, Kathy Flaherty, who said, "Disclosing a disability to an employer enables a person to live one's life authentically and be able to bring one's whole self to work." (4).[2] I have to one hundred percent agree with her on this. If there were no other reasons for you to follow through with this step, then I would say, *this is it*. You deserve to be just as comfortable as everyone else. If everyone else can come to work in their "real skin," then why can't you?

"Disclosure is divulging or giving out personal information about a disability."(3) In order to professionally and adequately disclose your disability, there are three things that you should be sure to cover in this disclosure. There is no single or wrong approach to disclosure, but if you tie in these three factors, you may end up with fewer questions because you answered concerns upfront. The three factors that should be disclosed are:

1. The nature of the disability,
2. How it may limit you,
3. If it can affect your ability to do your job and how.

I personally feel that the Federal Government is a great place to work for any physically challenged person. They allow special preference in the interview process for those that possess a Schedule "A" Letter (see item number 1 on the Resources page). They even create positions with disabled workers in mind and go the extra mile to accommodate them, without them having to demand what they need. It's incredible, and I encourage you to check out their USA jobs site.

As I have researched during years of job searching, I have learned that the Federal Government is trying to be an example for others. So, this is not entirely about our population, but the integrity of leadership and due diligence. They develop their workforce based on how they think that the country should run. With this in mind, their efforts are to influence the private sector to make the same efforts—tremendous stuff. As I said before, when it comes to private sector companies, you have to go the extra mile and do your homework before investing time into placing applications. Glassdoor is excellent at giving authentic feedback on company work environments.

Again, my question earlier was, "Who is really in the wrong here?" I will say this - how will people know what you need if you never tell them? And don't dare to answer that your employer is wrong if the company doesn't know the severity of your impairment. People aren't mind readers, and we should not expect them to be. It's just not a God-given talent.

In some ways, you may feel that it would make you more prone to discrimination when, in fact, you are isolating yourself from potential support. It took me so many years to learn this. In fact, hiding a part of yourself will take its toll on you (believe me, I have tried that as well). It is nerve-racking, walking a thin line and hoping people don't "discover it." It's not worth it.

I hope that this chapter has given you some insight into the changes that you need to make in your workplace, which will make it less of a stressful workday. You even now have resources in front of you for employers who have suited their companies for your needs. That should be great motivation to move in the direction of change and to know, once again, that you are not alone in this fight for equality in your workplace. I desire that those of us that harbor a hearing loss will learn to break out of this shell of silence. When this happens, we are prone to meeting others in our workplace who struggle with the same issues.

Once people see one employee thrive and attain the accommodations they need, it will hopefully create a domino effect within other companies where accommodations are requested more. That is my hope with this chapter; that you will apply it and enable yourself to operate at your best in the workplace, just as President Theodore Roosevelt and I did. A change from the fear of rejection has to happen; this first change has to happen internally. Change may be a tad bit difficult, but it's worth it, and you will love yourself for it.

People don't accept us until we first accept ourselves. So, stop viewing it as telling the entire world your deepest, darkest secret. It's just not that serious. It's about what's going to be best for you and helping you to overcome workplace dread.

If others can enjoy their day at work, then so can you!

CHAPTER 6

Kick Relationship Blues... Change How You Relate in Your Personal Relationships!

> *"Hearing loss puts pressure on social relationships by complicating the conversational exchange that is so crucial for forming social relationships."*
> —Tine Tjornhoj-Thompson and Hans Henrik Philipsen, Social Authors

It matters. it's as simple as that...

Relationships matter. Friendships matter. Parents matter. Children matter. Significant others matter. Every type of relationship we pursue is an expression of a desire to get to know others. It is what gives life itself its true essence, to convene and relate with others. In this chapter, I will be uncovering the truth behind our struggle to maintain relationships. I will be sharing useful tips that allow you to always be at your best in social settings!

I will be presenting conversations, conjugal partners, single life, clubs, movie theaters, choosing a partner wisely, and more! You will learn the whole nine yards to kicking relationship blues. We're even going to get down deep and dirty and discuss that little sad habit of intentionally acting as if you're not hearing others and the reasons that we sometimes withdraw from much-loved friends and family. This is a chapter that you will love because it will change your approach to relationships. We know, through living our daily lives, that this ability to socialize is so important. Communicating and socializing are the epitome of happiness in all of us. So, why not learn it and conquer, while wearing a smile!

Let's talk about conversational exchange for a moment. Conversational exchange can be described as listening closely and responding appropriately. When we truly master good conversational exchange, we listen and allow others to talk; we receive what they are saying, and we respond.

> *When we incorporate our lesser hearing into our lives, we tend to encounter feelings of frustration in social environments.*

I use the term "we" because both the lesser hearing suffer along with their loved ones. "Hearing loss disturbs this smooth 'give-and-take.'" The social situation is altered... the social complications resulting from hearing loss affect the temporal aspects of conversational exchange." (1).

On the flip side, we have to learn to take it a lot further than simple conversational exchanges and consider our tendency to wait to be invited into a conversation. This tendency for us to simply wait to be given our chance to talk springs from our tendency to miss pertinent information in conversations, and sometimes, we have to manage "in the moment" self-doubt; this produces internal frustration, and we dread that the overall conversational exchange will have less quality.

Not to sound like a trip to the audiologist, but this concept of self-doubt is fundamental because "studies show that hearing loss produces feelings of frustration, embarrassment, and distress for the partner and for the relationship in general." (4). [2]

There are some conversational exchanges, too, when we are at fault for an adverse outcome. Remember, the concept of conversational exchange is to listen and respond. If we are simply in a conversation for what we want to say and not fully receiving everything that was said, we are giving the short end of the stick; we are cheating or stepping on others—or whatever else we want to call it.

I tend to refer to it as "missing out on life" because we choose to avoid making an effort to hear the entire conversation. We allow "lazy ears," yet, we still want to be heard. We refuse to either figure out what was said or ask for things to be repeated. This manifests within us a feeling of unsureness that will continue to grow within us as we continue to practice this terrible habit. Even though you can establish a flow in conversations, we always want to assure ourselves that we have heard the entire conversation.

So, there you have it… a breakdown of a few tidbits that come with the lesser hearing communication. I just want to assure you that you are not alone, just as I have stressed throughout this book. Many are in a struggle, trying to avoid being seen as "selfish" (not listening to others) in their conversations. There is a balance that we must achieve, but most of us don't know the steps. Now that you are aware of this impact, if you genuinely want to be a part of better conversation exchanges, then you must be willing to change a few approaches to how you converse. This will improve your conversations.

Sometimes, we must make more effort to control conversations, other times, we may offer more compassion, and sometimes, you must simply listen. However, how can we do this when our ears cause us to miss out on chunks of information? Be my guest and read on.

How We Convey it is How They Will Receive it...

You would not believe what comes out of my mouth sometimes, while on the other end of the phone with friends, especially when I am unable to hear juicy conversations. In my desperate attempts to "save face," I have caused some confusion. I have assumed that they are frustrated after numerous attempts of repeating themselves, only because I am deeply embarrassed. I might say, "I'm so sorry, girl. You know I still didn't hear you," or "Okay, say it one more time, please."

It's like begging them to be patient. They aren't the impatient ones; however, it's always me getting uncomfortable about it. I'm outright assuming that people just don't (or won't) have the patience for me. Good friends will reel me right back in by saying something like, "Dominique, it's okay. What I was saying was _____." I even have a few friends that may say, "Hang on, check your text message. I just sent what I was saying to you." I check the text message, and the conversation continues.

We have to be aware of our accomplishments and build on them. We must celebrate the successful levels we attain with others and use that to our advantage.

There are moments in conversation exchanges when you will get stuck, but here's a question. Have you ever stopped to glorify those calls that continue to roll forth in peace, as you do hear the rest of the conversation? Have you ever rewarded yourself for "conquering" conversations that were absolutely flawless? We have to acknowledge these things. We have to be aware of our accomplishments and build on them. We must celebrate the successful levels we attain with others and learn from that. Sometimes, we may even sit down to a conversation with a negative expectation that we will not hear it. This is, by far, the wrong approach; this type of habit sets the pathway for happenings that you will not like. It's okay to tell loved ones, "Wait, I did not hear you."

If we must ask a person to repeat something, we must also account for how we ask for it—we must be graceful when we ask. In other words, consider the person's feelings and the fact that you are asking them to be patient with you. Try not to be uptight when you ask for help. In his book, "Don't *Sweat the Small Stuff,*" Richard Carlson states that "the root to being uptight is our unwillingness to accept life as being different in any way, from our expectations. Very simply, we want things to be a certain way, but they are not a certain way." (6) In other words, we were born this way, so quite simply, just drop the uptight approach to how you ask for help. Trust me, it works.

Think about this. During the conversation exchange process, when we come to these frustrating points, and a person is asked to repeat it, the tone of the deliverer's voice shifts. Sometimes, we receive this as if the deliverer is becoming agitated. After this occurs, the message is not delivered with its initial linguistic richness (or initial excitement); it's just delivered as reduced to what is necessary. What does this mean?

It means that there are emotions within that time-lapse of asking for a repeat of a thing or two. My point is that there are always communicators on both sides. When dealing with conversation adjustments, we must portray a positive image of expression. If, while making the request, you continue to smile and avoid drawing in negative energy, the person honoring your request will also remain calm; they may even make facial gestures to confirm that you are able to continue to hear the conversation.

We simply must become more aware. This allows us to be more conscious of our tone when we ask people for their help. We should desire to master this. Think about it, sometimes we need others to hear the ending statement to a movie, or when the waitress quotes the dinner specials. I promise you; this is a habit you will want to nail down. Using it with ease will help you to keep a leveled playing field!

People Have the Choice of Whether or Not to Assist Us

Although this is true, we want them to be open to helping us. We want them to feel good about this. As a high school teacher, I witnessed terrible accounts of young adolescents who could not get over their "sadness" to be helped. This blocked their abilities to socialize. One young man, in particular, was Eulus, who had a great personality. He was brilliant and loved to read the newspaper, including the comics; therefore, he always had an opinion or a story to share. He loved to lead the conversation, but he refused to listen and finish the dialogue with others, which can make people upset when they feel they listened to you, but you didn't return the favor and listen to them. Besides, everyone wants to be heard, right?

Sadly, Eulus was not even aware that he was never having well-balanced conversations. When he reached out to others to repeat things, they often brushed him off. How awful this must feel when you already have to be vulnerable enough to share with others when you have not heard something. I started to address each of Eulus' questions within the class when others wouldn't.

One day, he walked up to my desk at the end of the class period and asked, "Ms. Briscoe, why are people so two-faced with me?" He honestly felt as if people were being mean to him. But how could they be when they were listening to his stories? Something was missing. I asked him what he meant by this (but truly I already knew, but this is a teaching strategy that helps high school students to answer their questions; most of them will never accept your direct answer). He responded by saying that people smiled about his stories, but never repeated something for him when he didn't hear it. I explained the dynamics of a "give and take" within conversations and suggested that always leading the story wasn't getting their favor. "Have you shown them that you hear what they are saying?" I asked him.

He was silent and left for the day. The next day, he began assuring people that he was listening. He was now aware, and more classmates and friends began to open up, including him in conversations. His awareness was the start of more meaningful conversations. If we want friends and family to bless us, then we have to make an effort to show them we understand that love is a two-way street. Yes, love in life is a two-way street.

Eulus also decided to stop feeling sorry for himself and try. When we sit, sulk, and sigh, we cannot be the compassionate person others need for us to be; we just aren't in the mood. This kind of negative, crappy thinking is a dream killer; if you practice it, it must stop. We are a population that can only thrive on the sharing and caring of others. Embrace it;

become a part of it by doing your part by contributing to a happy society; in turn, you will be blessed.

Conjugal friction...

Conjugal relationships allow us to live and relate to others in our daily lives. It may be a dorm mate, an apartment roommate, a spouse or significant other, or a brother or sister. A hearing loss can put an enormous strain on conjugal relationships. In this section, I want to highlight a few things that you may already be aware of. I want to give you a few ways you can cope with them. I don't think that I am too much of a pain to live with, but you should probably ask the people that I have lived with in the past. Hahahahaha. Had to throw a joke in there. But seriously, I will just say that I have grown over the years.

In conjugal relationships, people eat, sleep, read, shop, mow the lawn, clean the house, go to church, watch TV, shower, clean the garage, trim the bushes, paint the house, repair the car, drop the kids off, etc. When we decide to share space with others, they will feel the bite of living with someone with lesser hearing. This worked out quite well for me for a few years as a young adult. As I noted earlier, I have a twin sister; she was my dormmate in college, and after college, we bought a house together. Talk about a life of luxury. We were joined at the hip—we came into life together and were determined nothing could stop or separate us.

Well, reality always sets in, doesn't it? We both started to pursue different interests. I was always with a real estate client or at church, and she was always with other friends or at events that I simply didn't favor. All of a sudden, the television was up too loud, or I talked on the phone too loud. We became irritated with each other as we grew apart. I love her, but our time of living together was officially up. So, I found her a home to purchase, and she moved out, while I stayed in the jointly purchased house.

I was finally living in my own perfect space until a few years later. I decided to enter into a monogamous relationship. He and I were very close and kept a very faithful relationship. However, this was a lesson to show me just how much he was affected by my hearing loss. It was truly a learning experience.

Living with a significant other showed me the amount of sacrificing that another does for you when they want you to be happy.

For instance, he knew there was a specific place to stand in the kitchen to talk to me while I cooked, or we always sat in the same place at the dinner table. He was pretty compliant with repeating things for me when we attended outings, and he was pretty good at intervening on my behalf. He talked at a level that was always conveyed well and made me laugh and smile a lot. He carried a voice that was deep with bass and easy to understand. He was also cooperative during conversations, whether I heard everything or not. This made me feel comfortable asking him to repeat himself.

I knew that I needed someone I could let my guard down with because my family always made my living environment easier. I needed a partner that could add to the ease of living that I had built for myself. And that he did. It was a great experience for me to see and know what I needed if I ever decided to get married; I had finally learned, through this relationship, that I was capable of being in a long-term relationship with a hearing loss.

When I was younger, I always assumed that my relationships would be like other relationships, but that was not the case. There is a lot of sacrificing to be done on the part of one who has a partner of such. Although it's rarely acknowledged, it's an adjustment for both people. After a few years, we were engaged and on to planning a wedding. However, my hearing loss was soon put to the test.

I had never before considered that, with a hearing loss, people would not always be one hundred percent transparent in relationships. What do I mean by this? It's quite simple, honestly. Either they are one hundred percent for a partner, or they are not. Hard times can test out any partner, but our partners have to sustain the ability to avoid losing patience and resorting to slander. This is a no-no.

I will admit that one of the reasons my relationship ended was that this person could not bear with my loss over the long haul. When financial problems arose, he grew tired and discouraged, which showed in his words and actions. He began to leave me to struggle alone at events, when he usually intervened. Later, he stopped joining me altogether at events (which was extremely difficult). There is a crucial point that I want to make here. He had become my accommodation at events; therefore, this was disheartening.

He began to make insulting remarks about my hearing loss when he was upset. I can still feel the intensity of his words in his angry moments, saying, "I didn't say that, see? You can't hear!" stretching the word "hear" burned me to my soul. I would deem it even more disheartening than many relationship factors (cheating, dishonesty, etc.). At the end of the day, it was a lack of respect for my hearing loss, something that I had spent my entire life building up.

I think that was the straw that finally broke the camel's back, making me reconsider whether I could still respect him. As he repeated that phrase, again and again, it pushed me farther and farther away from him. I tried to communicate how uncomfortable it was to be judged. I felt it was wrong for him to assume that our problems were arising because of my hearing loss. I was outright offended because he chose to use my hearing loss as a manipulative tactic. It was of no good use to explain. He regressed and stopped making further efforts toward improving the relationship, as he felt that I was "being difficult." But there was no difficulty on my part, just his lack of commitment to a partner suffering a hearing loss.

I want to clarify something for a moment… this is never okay. No matter what loss people suffer, there is always a way to say it. If our minds and lips cannot patiently coordinate and think about things before we say them, then maybe a partner with a hearing loss may not be the person for us. People dealing with a hearing loss, or any other physical loss, have a struggle within them every day; the last thing they need is a partner to woefully "confirm" their inadequacies.

Still today, I am not sure of what I missed that he referred to. I just know that, with the tone of his hurtful voice, I simply lost interest in even wanting to know. To hell with you, is what you begin to think when someone goes there on a hearing loss. Manipulation is used by men and women all of the time, but manipulating someone based on a physical loss, is simply not cool.

I decided to call off my wedding. It was a time that I was in deep communion with God about whether to marry, and God answered my prayers one day. I realized that I didn't have to marry him simply because we had a child together. I have no regrets about this relationship because I have a beautiful daughter.

I have now come to understand that people can never just misuse your state against you; it was the reason I decided to end my engagement with him—I didn't want my daughter to see her mother being mistreated. One motto I use all of the time, even to this day, is "kids do what they know." There will never be a day where my child will infer any "inadequacies" about my hearing loss, making my heartache, because I am not raising her like that. That was a reason for me to hit the ground running quickly.

Partners must be ready to share your journey and commit to it for the long haul.

I shared this journey of mine because that is just what this was for me… a journey. A journey can teach us many things; the most significant thing I learned from this relationship was that partners must be ready to share your journey, committing to it for the long haul. This means that this person has to be willing to be honest when it comes to your hearing loss. You need a partner who is truly up for that journey.

Things may go well initially with new people, but only time will tell if they have been patient enough to accept this part of you. So, before you enter into your next monogamous relationship, make sure that the confidence in your capabilities is an "A+." For years, I wasn't uncomfortable with him because I was confident in my abilities, but when he decided to deceive me, I was able to withstand him confidently. This ordeal didn't cause me to question myself, because yes, he knew me, but I knew myself too. In other words, I was at my best because I was aware of my capabilities.

I was able to withstand because I assured myself, continuously loved, and built myself up. I am assured of the lessons that I have learned, and my intent now is to ensure that future potential partners get their deserving fair chance, and for that reason, I have forgiven him.

If you struggle with a hearing loss, and this is your story (or one similar), then I encourage you to try forgiveness. Sometimes people simply aren't aware of the amount of pain they cause, especially hitting on a hearing loss. I would encourage this for your own healing. Holding onto the grudge of heated revenge for another person will not allow you to smile and ask others to repeat themselves. It will not let you be compassionate toward others in conversations, which you need to do. The inability to forgive wears us down, seeping through our skin like alcohol. People sense it, and they run from it. Never allow another person to have this much power over your life. Enough said!

Good and Bad Intervenors

In this section, we will discuss the role of an intervenor (for a person with lesser hearing) within personal relationships. The word "intervenor" involves assisting. The type of assistance that an intervenor would supply for a lesser hearing person would be encouragement, gestures, and repeating things. When someone intervenes for you, they provide you with assistance so that you are not conflicted. Significant others frequently provide this (without knowledge) to their partners. They may urge you to remove your shoes at a dinner party or repeat what the concert emcee asks the audience to do.

So, they don't resolve conflicts, but help us to avoid possible conflicts. Intervenors must be very well-bonded to another person to be of great assistance. Often, this cannot be done within the context of a first date, or such, because we have not learned people, their needs, and their habits yet. Intervenors are extremely valuable in our lives, but they must operate in honesty so that we are able to fully trust them when our ears miss something.

> *It is not until we stop, understand, and accept our hearing loss that we can begin to understand the power of such help in our lives.*

A caring intervenor doesn't ever want you to feel frustration. They want you to enjoy the trip to Italy just as much as they enjoy the trip. They want to help us along at events so that we can bask in our success and enjoy our accomplishments. That is a great intervenor. Research also shows the importance of "good" partners that intervene. As I am writing and researching this, I cannot wrap my head around the fact that I had not thought of this while I was in relationships years ago. However, it is not until we stop, understand, and accept our hearing loss that we can begin to understand the power of such help in our lives. I did run into this problem a few times in relationships, yet I had the answer right in front of me. They were just not people who thought that far into my needs.

There are many ways that I could view it, but the truth is, there are many bad intervenors. I mean, they really suck. Once you've had a few good partners who do this well, you will begin to see when a person is a no-go. They may know, process, and understand all that you need, and still leave you in the dark with what's going on, because they simply don't have the desire to care that much for another. This is what I need you to understand. A certain level of maturity is so vital!

Don't be so quick to believe the hype that "people who care will still be there for you in your time of need." You need someone who honestly cares about themselves, and they, in turn, will care about you. This can be a sensitive issue for some of us; who can I trust to convey what was said? Who can I trust to refrain from rude facial gestures when I don't hear something? Who can I trust to be mature enough to put their feelings aside and understand that intervening is a significant part of my living and well-being? I could go on and on here, but I think that you get the picture.

One struggle between partners of lesser and regular hearing is the failure to understand how lesser hearing people process information. This inability to understand can cause problems and irrational behavior on the part of both people. "Spoken interaction... depend on the ability of the speakers-hearers to coordinate their actions temporally, so as to produce talk that unfolds by turn with a minimum of gap or overlay." (5) To understand the long pause for understanding and replying for the hearing disabled person, one needs to recognize that it is a termed, temporal coordination, and it deals with the temporal lobe of the brain. The temporal lobe houses the auditory cortex, which makes sense of what is received into the brain. It's the little factory that processes units into meaningful units, such as speech and words.

Blah, blah, blah. I am saying that partners need to understand that we may require things to be repeated or be given extra time to process, making sense of what we heard. This is the jibber jabber of it all. When partners understand this, then they will flourish. They must understand how the brain works. They must also understand that giving you more time or repeating things is of great help.

The best trait of a great partner is care. When people care, they will be patient. When they don't care, they will make a minimal effort, hoping that you don't need much. This is not rocket science; it's a clean and clear approach if you think about it. It can be understood by simply asking yourself a few questions. How does your mate take your feelings into account? Are they responsive to your hearing needs? Do they ask you about the struggles you encounter while having lesser hearing? If not, then you may continue to receive minimal efforts from them regarding your hearing loss. Never expect that someone will simply have compassion because you need to hear something. Instead, surround yourself with people who care, to avoid encountering hurt feelings.

Lowering your standards will hurt in the long run...

It's amazing how quickly we are to sacrifice something we need in relationships when we find a companion that we truly want it to work with. We convince ourselves that it will be alright, we can live without it, it's not a big deal. Well, this may be the case for some standards, but when it comes to a hearing loss, I strongly advise against it. Providing you with these things is a choice that your partner has to make. It will take someone compassionate, understanding, and extremely patient over the long haul.

Let's just put all of the cards on the table, shall we? Let's just look at this for what it is. This is the person that you will be (over the long haul)… attending family outings, graduations, weddings, and all sorts of social events for years to come.

And, if you have big dreams, then this is the person who will accompany you to receive awards and travel to foreign countries with you. We just can't afford to take this decision lightly.

In his book *"Straight Talk, No Chaser,"* Steve Harvey embraces the importance of choosing a mate well. He says: "What's not okay is burying what you want and need for security, protection, respect, and support. Yielding and bending to his [or her] will—pushing aside what you want is compromising. And when you compromise who you are for a man [or woman], there is no way you can find deep, long-lasting happiness. If you're not happy, you're not loving him [or her] the way he [or she] needs to be loved."

The same goes for aligning this mate with your hearing needs and letting them know your standards. This is a *support factor*. That's right. Just as you let them know that they have to treat you to dinner at least twice a month and send flowers occasionally, you also need to tell them to "keep me afloat" at outings. In a sense, they need to become one with you and understand that there will be times when you will need them to jump in there and help out; if you miss a beat, without making a scene of it, and keep it as low key as possible.

You should let them know your needs and how you operate to see if they are up for the challenge. Some are not, and that's okay. They are not the one for you. You cannot afford to sacrifice this. From years of dating, I have learned firsthand that some people are up for the challenge. When people meet you initially, they do see a hearing aid, but many want to still get to know you. They will put aside the need to know every little detail about it at first and ask a question here or there as the relationship develops. While they are getting to know you is the best time to make your needs known so that there are no misunderstandings.

I mean, let's face it, before this book, had you ever actually taken the time to realize and analyze how complicated "going out" or "dating" was for you? Maybe you have. Do you really think a regular hearing person has developed an understanding of this if you have not yet shared anything with them? Nope. Not at all, and it is an issue that could definitely make or break a relationship.

What can also make or break a relationship is telling "too much, too soon" about your hearing loss. Knowing how much to share is trivial. We don't want to overwhelm people. I have had my share of doing this to people; it's disheartening when people have not gotten the chance to get to know you first. When you ask people to assist you, you must walk them through some steps and talk with them about it. Give them some time to process it (but not too much time). It shouldn't be a hard decision for a partner because it is something that you need. But you do have to give a person a minute to process all that you are asking them to do.

There is nothing more comforting than avoiding the struggle of social outings, and there is no better partner than one who supplies this.

Making sure that your chosen companion (because he or she is chosen, and you are a gem to have) is ready to intervene is very important. Yes. You do need this. I need it. I needed it earlier in my life, I need it now, and I will need it when I get older. That is what I mean by the "long haul." People change over time. That is a given in life. But this cannot change. This is why you require true and authentic real love. Love that sustains. In a loving relationship, this habit will become second nature to your partner because they want to learn how to best help you. Without love, this will be a struggle, and you will find yourself begging for what you asked for upfront.

Your hearing loss will be there with you for the long haul, just as your beautiful smile, long or short legs, light or dark skin. It is a part of who you are that's not going anywhere, and their patience with it can't go anywhere. Once you have a partner who does this second nature (and for the long haul), you are home free, and you've got another great reason to love your partner wholeheartedly.

Let me just address one thing as it pertains to partners. In this chapter, I addressed confidence. In this situation of expecting someone to speak up for you, you have to possess the right amount of confidence to speak up for yourself, too. Let's face it… no matter how great a partner you have, not many will intervene if your confidence slacks.

Most partners are pretty much going to do for you as much as you do for yourself. Some will coddle and spoil to encourage you to press on, but even this "extra attention" gets old after a while. If they see you shying away from the group, they may assume that you don't want to hear. There are many different ways in which couples coexist. But with our partners, we have to have a "oneness" in which they can pick up how we are feeling and what we need.

If they are just not that into you, then this will never happen. If you both have not reached a certain point in your relationship when you are both vulnerable, this may be difficult. When others see us being confident, they will be confident for us, as well. This is the challenge that comes with lesser hearing. For this reason, there is a book that I would encourage you to read. It's a short and easy-to-read book with great insight called "How to Make People Like You in 90 Seconds". It addresses everything from a handshake to eye contact, to verbal cues.

Perhaps a little confidence booster wouldn't be a bad idea before you stepped out on your next date or invited your mate along for another awards dinner. In this book *How to Make People Like You in 90 Seconds*, the author, Nicholas Boothman says, "As you meet and greet new people, your ability to establish rapport will depend on four things: your attitude, your ability to "synchronize" certain aspects of behavior; like body language and voice tone, your conversation skills and your ability to discover which sense (visual, auditory, or kinesthetic) the other person relies on most." (reference). Doesn't that sound useful, now that you have decided to let your guard down and pep up your step?

Don't Lose Your Spunk When Dating and Mingling...

Attending outings is not a particularly relaxing time for us. That is what many others have to begin to realize with empathy. For the normal hearing person, it's a great idea. "Yes, let's do it! Let's all hang out after work!" But for the lesser hearing person, there is so much preparation that goes into the process, between arriving on the scene and packing up to leave the event. Coping with a hearing loss is about managing noise. We can admit that the 'management of noise' factor is a lot easier just sitting on the couch and adjusting the volume to the television, than attending happy hour.

It's much easier to choose to stay at home. Going out begins with: The dreaded telephone conversation to confirm the hangout spot and location, the dark and quiet drive across town at night (darkness minimizes our senses that enable us to see, which we really count on), the arrival and analyzing the room (hoping the crew didn't choose a table beside the band), the watching of body language to assure we feel the vibe of the scene upon entrance (sometimes people whisper, but body language can give you negative or positive vibes and increase your awareness for heightening your other senses), the pulling up of the chair and greeting everyone at the table, in hopes of not missing a new name (this can have you in your thoughts for a few minutes, trying to guess a name), the low talking waitress asking what you are drinking (which makes you request whatever comes to mind while others order "maxed out" drink specials), the multiple conversations across a table, to which only the nearest one to you is even accessible, and the list goes on. So, you tell me again, which is the easier option?

Think about it, we're being asked to voluntarily "suffer through" getting ready and getting to the event, only to keep asking others to repeat themselves. No wonder we often pass. For me, it's a 50/50 because I am somewhat of an introvert. I have learned to shrug off bad happenings as part of the process, and the less attention I give them, the better off I am. Sometimes it's okay to say, "I made it here. Who cares about the hassle before? That's over and done with, on goes the night, let's have fun!"

What can be uplifting is arriving at events and seeing great friends that intervene for you, who are ready to service your needs. They pull up beside you and say, "Did you hear what we were talking about?" This helps you to relax and make it a great night! It also makes the frustrating preparation worth it because, in the end, we all want to feel loved and included, right?

The Joke is Gone...

Ever hear the statement, "the joke is gone" from a sarcastic family member or co-worker? It burns me up. We sometimes are faced with the case of missing the spontaneity of a joke. Yes, jokes are spontaneous. When we converse with others, then jokes can come up spontaneously. Sometimes, missing even a small part of a joke (such as a name or time of day) so trivial to making everyone laugh can be disheartening; we can all admit that laughter is one of life's best energies, especially within a group. Here's an example: Dave tells everyone at the table, "My sister, Lindsey, walked into a tall lamp last night at 3:00 a.m. and woke the entire house up." That's a joke that is bound to get some energy going. But if you didn't hear the time (3:00 in the morning), then you may start to think *why was everyone asleep, anyway?*

As for myself, I always want to know the joke, but there were times in my younger life that I regressed and simply let it go. Then I noticed I was unhappy with not being included. So, now, I've learned to simply chuckle along and kindly ask, "What time was it that she walked into the lamp?" Here's a thought, and you probably have experienced it: Someone will yell out, "3:00 a.m.," but another person may say, "Oh, sorry you missed it." That is missing the spontaneity.

In this area, I would advise you to consider what you would prefer and try that for a little while. If you are okay with dismissing the joke and finding your entertainment with the group in other ways, then that is fine. On the other hand, asking strengthens your level of inner confidence, and continued practice of this habit will cause it to become easier over time.

This is one of those issues that depends on where you are in your life and how comfortable you are with others knowing about your hearing loss. Your level of confidence is so important when dealing with others. It has to be continually strengthened, so why not try it surrounded by familiar faces? Get used to asking around friends and family and endure the joy of others looking out for you. Laugh along, smile, and say thank you after they have done so.

Whether you want to ask for jokes to be repeated also depends on whether you are familiar with everyone, and I mean everyone in the group. Sharing this with unfamiliar people heightens your risk of being judged, insulted, or even dismissed. So, to examine the crowd of people that you are among is extremely important as well. Is this a professional crowd, or just a young hangout group that cracks jokes and insults on each other? The latter group has never received a request to repeat a joke from me, personally.

We live in a time of speak up or get walked over.

I will be honest; sometimes, my hearing aid is a "show off" gadget, especially when I come upon "those who stare" or "hearing aid stalkers." The thrill of "showing off" is what inspires me to wear my hearing aid with pride. Do you ever come upon people in a gathering that continually stare at your hearing aid? Well, sometimes, I actually "push back" and burst their bubble. If I am in a staff meeting and come upon this, I make sure to raise my hand and give my intelligent input. Or, I will ask a very good question. This helps me to be perceived as smart and not merely limited to a loss; my thought is, "whatever gives me poise as these idiots keep staring," and that's what I will do.

Most of the time, if you give your comment (or raise a question within the group) and turn directly to the "hearing aid stalkers," after with a sharp eye, they will back up. Remember, people only possess the power that you give them. Girl, please! Back up! The keen eye does the trick every time. And no, I am not making a sharp eye at you because I am unhappy with my lack of hearing. My boldness is there because you have the audacity to keep staring. I know that this is not everybody. But I can say it is where we need to be. It is an excellent example of the confidence that we must exert. This life is no joke. We live in a time of "speak up or get walked over." I'm not encouraging you to bash people that stare at your hearing aid, but there is nothing wrong with a tweak in body language so that they will get the message: "You can stop staring now."

The point is that, in social settings, you will have to figure out what your approach will be and test it out for a while to make sure that it suits you. If you have decided to dismiss a lot of group jokes, be sure that you are happy that way. If you choose to ask others to repeat jokes, then be sure that you are ready for some rude responses here and there, and then get over it. Go home and write about it in your emotional journal, go to sleep, and wake up to another day. The more you practice this approach, your ability to act will become more natural over time, and you will be happy… but again, you have to figure it out.

Three Strikes and You're Out

Sometimes, people are running from place to place while on the go when they make a request of you. Just because you have a hearing loss doesn't mean you can't grab a bag of groceries from the car or help to stir spaghetti sauce. However, because they have asked in a quick, panicking way, then you may have missed what they asked you to do. This causes you to become frustrated and resentful of the way they are talking to you.

Remember that, while they may be shouting, please be compassionate when others hurriedly ask you to do something; it will take some patience on your part. I have learned that it is best to help them for now and then approach them once they have calmed down; then, tasks are completed.

Great relationships flourish on basic respect.

Let them know that you find it a bit offensive that they shout orders at you, and that it would be best for them to find a way to stand still, look directly at you to get your attention, and then make the request. Take a minute to observe their actions and see if they are taking in what you are saying. They have to process what you are saying, or this will lead to continued frustration for you. Remember, people do what they know, and they treat you how you allow them to.

Give them a chance by showing them that you can be patient. But don't give too many opportunities to people who don't know how to request something without hollering. If you don't set boundaries with people in these kinds of situations, then it will become the norm, and they will think that it is okay to shout because you never spoke up about it. I don't even have to ask you the question of whether you have experienced this. I know that you have, and it is gut-wrenching.

Great relationships flourish on basic respect, and this is one of those times. If a person is determined to speak at high levels when you have told them that it is unnecessary, take that as a sign of carelessness or even sarcasm. Either way, it's not good. Good friends process our needs and what we are asking of them. They don't go against the grain of what works for us. That just doesn't make sense.

Many times, when dealing with sarcastic people, they may be talking "under their breath" about happenings, but you don't catch it. Trust me… don't make the time for people like this in your life. Personally, this is a habit that gets under my skin. In high school, I had a few friends that always wanted to talk about other people under their breath. I stopped friending them altogether because I simply couldn't trust them, and better yet, if they ever spoke under their breath about me, I would have no idea, and would not be given a proper chance to defend myself. I will say this: anyone who cannot talk at a level for you to hear everything while knowing about your hearing loss should be out the door. Period!

We have to always be aware of our surroundings and make sure that people are not inflicting their pain onto us or making a field day of our situation. Hey, it's life, and it does happen. It can happen at the club or among immature co-workers. My point is that when you have brought things to their attention, you can only allow them a certain amount of chances. You will, eventually, either blow up at them or take in an insult. Either way, it is not good for you.

I live by the "Three strikes, and you're out" rule. However, sometimes some people don't even deserve that. Some people may only want to be your friend because they think they can control you, and somehow, this makes them look better. They act as if they are helping you when they are hindering you. Be very careful with people like this; learn to pick up on people's intentions. It will save you from a lot of hurt and pain.

The wonderful thing is, as we grow older, picking up on these traits in other people tends to increase. It is a skill that we master over time. We need to continually watch others' actions and body language; our eyes are our biggest protectors. I wear glasses; I would not dare to step outside of the house, or even the bedroom without them.

I've shared with you before how reading body language and attitudes have helped me a lot in my adolescent years. Well, as I grew older, I thoroughly mastered it; and I encourage you to do this as well. Take a longer look at body language and learn to use it to your advantage. In my life, it has worked wonders.

The Act of Intentionally Not Hearing

As a young adult during my twenties, nothing other people said mattered. I had this habit of "hearing when I wanted to", if that makes sense. You know exactly what I am talking about. It's just one of the "'toy gimmicks" of having a hearing loss", but it's also a little rude. In this practice, we may not want to hear, and in our stubbornness, we don't want to make an effort to hear, so the act of not hearing is used intentionally against another. It's cruel, unacceptable, and distressing. It tarnished a few of my relationships during those years.

Rejection comes in many forms.

This act can actually cause mistrust and distance. Playing games doesn't work for any type of relationship. When we play games and use our hearing disability against other people, it really can be hurtful and hard for them to forgive. People may even question how, or why, you would do that and wonder if all who harbor a hearing loss do this from time to time. In other words, it places an image of "lack of integrity" on our community. However, if you're reading this book, I am going to assume that you are not on that path because you are making an effort to learn coping strategies, such as those offered in this book, and I am proud of you.

Whether relationships are between people who are hearing disabled or regular hearing, everyone deserves our honesty. In fact, if you tend to play this card, consider talking more with counselors and specialists, so that you can express to them the loss bothers you enough to provoke the desire to tune everyone out. Rejection comes in many forms. In my case, some days, I was just overwhelmed, and I didn't want to talk to anyone. If this is the case, then say it. Our ears perform double the work, so sometimes we can lose energy when we have not done much.

When times get overbearing, then communicate to your loved ones that you have taken your hearing aids out for the night to give your ears and mind a rest. It's a much better approach to say, "they have been irritating my ears sometimes", instead of placing the feeling of rejection onto others.

Pace Yourself and Be Mindful of Loud Environments...

Loud environments can be overwhelming. If you have to stress too much just to be heard and you still barely hear anything, maybe it's better for your health to simply relax from any conversation and enjoy the scenery. I have had plenty of nights when I decided that it was best to do this, particularly at the club scene, which is known for its loud music, dramatic and perky patrons, and the inability sometimes to talk, even among regular hearing people. I would simply relax, enjoy the scene, and add my two cents here and there. It just feels more like the right thing to do, since my struggle is hearing.

Over time, I found that it was just not worth it. Maybe it's my own experience, but I found that the more I shouted, the more I didn't pick up on dangerous happenings going on around me. Some environments are not worth multitasking because you may need your eyes to be safe. In other words, it's not always a bad thing to sit back and monitor your surroundings. It could be the chance for your eyes to pick up something that your ears didn't.

Staying aware of your environment is one of the greatest factors of always being at your best. Observing is an undervalued skill. Going to a movie doesn't require the exchange of conversations, but the volume of most cinemas should be against the law. And to think that I am saying this as a lesser hearing movie patron. Sounds crazy, right? My approach to this is to always turn my hearing aid down and simply use the captioning devices. Most of the time, if I can decrease the volume on my hearing aid, then I can still hear it at a reasonable level. This is something regular level hearing movie patrons cannot ever do, and it is a blessing for us in these loud movie theaters. Merely living as a person who is aware of what's harmful to their health and staying clear of these things, is a blessing. Having a hearing loss allows you to do this. Actually, it makes you do it!

The Riff Raff of Lesser Hearing...

Researching a few sources, I came upon quite a few interesting points, which helped me to better understand all of the riff raff faced by our population when it comes to building and maintaining relationships and conversational exchange. A study presented in 2018 by Hearing Review Online, (2) found that "coping with hearing loss is basically about managing noise; this is being able to pick out the relevant and sense-making sounds from irrelevant noise" and quite frankly, I could not have said this better myself.

One husband who had a wife with hearing loss said, "I cannot have a conversation with ___ on a train or in a public place, because we are continually being bombarded with announcements, noise, and background music that totally preclude conversation."(3).

What he describes is a situation of (being a partner to the lesser hearing spouse) having a hard time even forming a conversation with so much noise in the environment. I find this to be particularly true. My twin sister—who is hearing disabled—actually stops me from talking to her, if her kids are yelling in the background, or if the fire truck drives by. We both just sit and wait for the noise to subside. We know that it's not worth the struggle.

> *Failure to communicate will create unintentional pain, which leads to resentment in partners.*

This is another reason to be patient with partners and show them how to be patient with you. Knowledge is so very powerful, and if a person knows that you simply will not hear in the midst of so much noise, then I doubt if they will keep trying to force you to listen. They will wait until you are more comfortable with communicating and go from there. This is why you must communicate your needs. There are so many traits and habits that can wreak havoc on our relationships. Just imagine being married twenty years to a partner that never knew that you could not hear fire trucks, yet always kept talking amid them.

That is twenty years of frustration; all because you choose not to sublet information about what you need. Imagine a partner who doesn't know you don't prefer clubs and loud places, yet keeps having birthday parties in the same spots every year. Continually experiencing this type of unintentional pain will cause resentment. It's a snowball effect when living with this loss, and the more our partners know, the better. The more we bond with our partners, the more willing and able they are for us, the more we will let our guard down and tell them what we need. This will help us to avoid having to end bad relationships and experiencing hurt feelings.

As we close out this chapter, there is a lot that I want you to take from it, but what you must start to do is tell people what you need. Also, practice compassion, and others will have compassion for you. That is how you build strong, reliable relationships.

CHAPTER 7

Kick These Six Habits: Change What Works Against Your Own Self-Love!

> "Change will not come if we wait for some other person, or some other time. We are the ones we've been waiting for. We are the change that we seek."
> —Barack Obama, Former POTUS #44

LET'S FACE IT! LIVING a lesser hearing life is a full plate in itself. In fact, I will shout it to the moon and back one thousand times: "I've got enough on my plate already." Part of making this change in your life will be based on how well you understand your daily habits, and how they may be working for you or against you!

These habits can be as simple as forgetting a pot of tea on the burner because we didn't hear it, or continuously listening to earbuds, unaware that we are decreasing our hearing capacity! So, in this chapter, I want to share my most crucial habits to avoid. And yes, I know there are a lot of others, and that will be presented in later books, but for now, I just want you to become acceptant with the concept that your daily habits do influence your life, and that they influence it tremendously!

Habit #1: Stop Procrastination

Wikipedia defines procrastination as "the avoidance of doing a task that needs to be accomplished by a certain deadline. It could be further stated as a habitual, or intentional delay starting or finishing a task, despite knowing it might have negative consequences."

> *If we are delaying doing what is important to us, as we tend to do when we procrastinate, then that shows us that something is wrong.*

Habit #1, procrastination, we know, is not categorized as a "hearing habit" in particular, but it is birthed from the family of "bad well-being habits". Now, you probably feel as if it's entirely up to you, whether you want to procrastinate in your life or not. Hear me when I say that "living with a hearing impairment doesn't allow us to procrastinate in our lives." Did you get that? Let's be real, unless your hearing aids are top-notch, $20k per hearing aid, you are probably going to gesture for people to repeat themselves; there has to be an amount of time allotted for waiting on people to repeat themselves.

So, now add procrastination to that, and what do you have? That's right, poor use of time. Or in the work world, you have a boss who would eventually write you up as an employee with an inefficient use of time or one who does not manage time wisely; those such write-ups often push us to the bottom of the employee pool, all because of our hearing levels. That is what we must avoid with all our might because it puts us at the opposite end of the spectrum for being at our best.

> *Procrastination is too much to risk when we already receive information in bits and chunks, while everyone else walks away fully knowledgeable and aware.*

Let me give you an example. Say that you are working a job with a technical team, and the team decides to call an emergency staff meeting ASAP, in the east wing of the building, next to the large warehouse, in a room with no microphones. Do you see where I'm going with this? The room setup will cause a few questions for you to be sure that you can adequately cover all that was presented during the meeting. And remember, this is an emergency meeting, so all information shared is vital to immediate productivity!

Do you really have time at moments like these, to sit around and feed your habit of procrastinating? Nope, not at all. If you're aiming to be a superb worker, then you will probably, at this point, review your meeting notes a few times, follow-up with colleagues, and consistently check your email every thirty seconds for any notes sent by senior advisors. At least that's what I would be doing. I would not dare to be procrastinating. It's too much to risk when we already receive information in bits and chunks, while everyone else walks away fully knowledgeable and aware all of the time. That is the norm that is expected in some workplaces; those of us with lesser hearing should plan accordingly. These types of occurrences are just bound to happen from time to time.

There is no perfect day. There are not many easy days, as this is life. Occurrences happen. Life happens. While we are on the topic of procrastination, I will also touch on the fact that it simply encourages laziness. Why is this such a bad thing? Well, because in everything that you do, once people see a hearing aid, you are representing the population of the lesser hearing. No, it's not fair, but it is the way of the world. Some people do stereotype certain populations. They may say things like "all blind people are rude", or "all deaf people are mean". We know that this is just not true. I have met some pretty rude hard of hearing people, as well as some kind and nurturing hard of hearing people. My point is, *represent well.* Procrastination plants the seed for laziness.

> *A bad habit is a bad habit,*
> *no matter if it's purchased or free of charge.*

I will admit that in certain phases of my life, I have been a heavy procrastinator. There was simply no drive to meet deadlines or get things done. What a risky way to live, I might add. I was thrilled and comfortable, just sitting and wasting time. Why did I do this? Well, it was a part of situational depression. It's difficult to explain, but procrastination can be as comfortable as having a drink. Let's face it… a bad habit is a bad habit, no matter if it's purchased or free of charge. Anything that's not challenging your mind and intellect is a bad habit.

However, I have to admit that procrastination has to be the worst habit of them all. Why? Because you are wasting time; tomorrow is not guaranteed. I look back on my life, and I am utterly ashamed. Tasks on my To-Do list were barely completed, I was continually calling others and bothering them, or I simply came up with any reason to not finish something, no matter how big or small. There was a strong sense within me that these things just were not important.

Depression can do this to us; however, it is not an excuse for my chronic procrastination, but I would encourage you that if you find yourself being too much of a procrastinator, it's evident that you are not taking the risk of not getting things done seriously. You may very well want to try counseling, too—just a thought. It worked out pretty well for me. I needed someone to speak to without feeling judged. People tend to place an "unworthy" interest in counseling, but nothing could be further from the truth. The truth is I was worthy of being heard. I was worthy of having my insurance pay someone to listen to my crap, as I dug myself out of the hole I had made in my life.

All of us, at some point in our education, came across the integer line. I placed a picture of it below. What I want you to see is what happens when you procrastinate, and how it eventually pushes you further left towards the negative integers. You don't move backward or forward at first; however, as procrastination habits grow, so does the effect that they have on your life. So, suddenly you're missing more deadlines and barely completing anything. If you look at your progress on the integer line you can see that your habits are causing you to fall behind and come out on the negative side of the integer line.

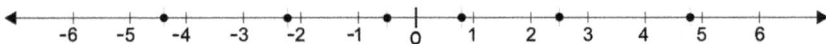

I love this visual because it helps me to understand simple common sense. The truth is, we can wallow in self-pity and regret for a time, but after a while, it has run its course, and it's time to suck it up and move on. Truthfully, no one wants to hear it except for a counselor, of course, which is what saved my poor soul. It took me a while to get back to "o" (on the integer line), which would be a neutral middle ground on this bar. It does take some time, effort, and self-love to pull yourself out of the habit of procrastination.

However, procrastination is a habit that can be broken with a bit of creativity and index cards. Here is a suggestion: Make four columns on an index card. Within each column, place one task that needs to get done this month. Then, each week, complete one task. Why only one task per week, you ask? My answer, baby steps when we are dealing with changing bad habits. You see, with procrastination, in our minds, we are comfortable in these states, so we need something to trigger the happiness that is derived from getting things done; these index cards will do that, and consistently, which is even more powerful. Every Saturday, check off one task for each week, then reward yourself at the end of the month. Next month, try for eight tasks a month (two per week) or move at your own pace. The point is that you will begin to see achievement and progress (on paper), and once again, be proud of yourself. Remember what I stated when I started this section, "If we are delaying what is important to us, as we tend to do when we procrastinate, then that exhibits carelessness, and something is wrong." Just think about it. Now, moving on!

Habit #2: Stop rushing from place to place and focus

The power of "coming back to center" is an awesome feeling. Years ago, I decided to conquer Habit #2, and that was to stop rushing through life. Life is not a marathon or a microwave meal! The decision to slow down didn't come easy, though. I never care to admit it, but it came as a result of a life-threatening accident that flipped a switch in my head to make me say, "I am no longer rushing around for anyone."

I had suffered a terrible accident because I simply was not making enough time in the morning to get to work on time. After this happened, I decided to plan better and to be honest with myself. Being honest with myself meant allowing myself to arrive late, until I could get up the gall to get places on time. It was the year that I eventually got fired; with that adjustment came setbacks of untimely arrivals, but I always say that I would rather lose my job than my life.

In order to acknowledge our intuition, we must slow down.

It was atrocious living back then. The feeling of rushing out the door, rushing to place my child in a car seat, rushing to get in the car, rushing to place my coffee cup, rushing to turn the key, rushing to fasten seatbelts, and rushing to drive off; and, as if that wasn't bad enough, rushing all the way to daycare to drop off my daughter and rushing all the way to work. I mean, really people, are we ever going to stop and listen to our intuition? My intuition has literally saved my life, I have learned. So now I use it much more.

It was fall, and my daughter, who was five years old at the time, had asked to switch her car seat to the center back seat; thankfully, I obliged because the opposing driver crashed directly into that very side from which she had moved. The thought of it makes me cringe to this day. However, it does show me that I was at a time where I was aligning my life with my intuition.

Our intuition has to be tapped into and acknowledged to be of use to us. In order to acknowledge it, we must slow down. Eagerness is a terrible encounter and a hectic way to live; eager to get to work on time, eager to jump into the fast lane, eager to get parked by 7:25 to clock in by 7:30. Wow, and to think that some people continuously practice these awful habits, almost every day of their lives, never for a minute understanding harm's way and the tragedies that they subject themselves to.

My "rushing era" was a time in my life that I probably struggled to hear the most; I would almost bet that this is the case for many others with lesser hearing. A rushed eager life will not stop and listen to intuition. Intuition could bless us and tell us to slow down. Slowing down, relaxing, and breathing slower would allow our vessels to open up, and along the way, our ears would open up. Oh, did you not know that? Avoiding the habit of rushing from place to place draws you closer to stillness so that you can exist closer to a mode of meditation. It allows you to accomplish twice as much with a clearer head. How so? Well, first, there is the fact that being lesser hearing, we tend to use our eyes more. This means that rushing puts a strain on our eyes. It's a major imbalance to call on our bodies to carry the stress and strain for our low hearing ears, but it is the truth. Do you come upon headaches if you happen to rush about without your hearing aids? Of course, you do; your body has to keep up.

It's the same as a broken leg. You receive a cane to walk so that you're able to balance both legs to avoid placing too much pressure on the uninjured leg. That is just the reality. So, let's make meditation our cane, our balance. What makes this approach so special is that we have no control over our eye's assertiveness when acting in place of our ears. It is truly a habit that I have tried to control myself and couldn't. It's quite funny, actually. A few years ago, an audiologist was amazed at how much I get done in a day, and then he asked me about my energy levels.

He brought to mind that, even though I was getting things done, I was exhausting my eyes and my other senses with the imbalance of my ears. This is why it is imperative to also wear two hearing aids. That's another story, but the point is this: Being lesser hearing, we don't have the power to stop our other senses from working in place of our ears, and this will happen when we are rushing around in chaos. Are you following? I hope so because the gesture to stop rushing from place to place (especially being hard of hearing) can save your life.

A strain on your eyes produces a strain on your head, which produces headaches, migraines, dehydration.

If you won't do it for yourself, then do it for the people who love you. Tell them, "I need a minute more to get there," or let them know, "I will meet you at the mall." I had to tell my sister that I would meet her at the mall to Christmas shop with her. No, never in a million years will you get me to drive speeding ahead at seventy miles per hour. Nope. Not going to happen. My mind may be able to keep up and even my eyes (which will receive a lot of pressure), but definitely not my ears.

Give it a try—slow down, stop rushing. The people around you will be proud of you, I promise, especially if you tell them why you decided to slow down. You can say, "I don't hear as well when I rush, so I have to slow down," and any loving friend or acquaintance should be able to respect and appreciate that. It's a lifesaver… a delicate lifesaver. Delicacy is a good thing. A strain on your eyes produces a strain on your head, which produces headaches, migraines, dehydration. The next thing you know, you are feeling totally out of sync from rushing to work, yet you haven't even gotten the day started. How do you focus in, anyway, after such rushing? How do you start a day at your best when you are already exhausted? It can be a difficult thing to do.

God forbid your supervisor comes rushing around the corner, giving important news, and you don't hear a thing because you are trying to focus. These things happen, you know. That is why I would encourage you to meditate. Meditation will get you into the habit of slowing down. Your thoughts move through your mind slower, and after twenty minutes of sitting and breathing, your physical body operates slower. Slower, but still efficient. This is possible because you will have cleared the clutter in your mind and focused only on what is important.

Habit #3: Stop wishing that it didn't exist

I think that we all would love to have access to the genie in a bottle and wish our problems away. Wouldn't that be the perfect Christmas gift to receive? Here's a thought: Do you look at your circumstances as a curse or a blessing? My own opinion of genies has always been that they are illusional characters that allow you to wish away your problems in areas you don't want to deal with, or to spread a magic carpet in front of you to whisk you away to the world that you want. Sorry friend, life just doesn't work like. Besides, would there be any strength gained if all of your problems dissolved for you? Even if the metaphor was used as a tool, it would only be employed by the weak-minded and those who could not deal with their problems. And really, who wants to be that person? I mean, yes, an easier life is a better life, but what could you really take credit for if you never conquered your own problems?

A life void of triumph is not one well-lived.

The thrill of accomplishing things is a powerful internal high that no person, drug, alcohol, or money can grant you. You did this! That's the takeaway. "Yes, I did that." Is that what you want to be able to say afterward? I defeated those who put me down about my hearing disability. I overlooked sarcastic, rude comments about my hearing. I stop taking to heart the fact that others had great hearing and that my hearing is not perfect. All of these thoughts and conquering them leads you to stop wishing for something that will never happen. You were either born lesser hearing, or you came upon it in your life, at some point. There is nothing wrong with working with it, but to wish that it didn't exist is only delaying dealing with reality. A live void of triumph is not one well-lived.

If you just learn to deal with it, then you will experience your full potential. That's the reality. There, I've given you a compelling reason that should move you to deal with it. The feeling of conquering something is a great feeling. Getting a driver's license is a great feeling, or passing an exam is a great feeling. Learning to play an instrument is a great feeling, or starting a new job is a great feeling. So, why not overcome your lesser hearing and receive the awesome feeling that this will bring you? When I say to overcome it, I don't mean stripping you of your lesser hearing state, but equipping yourself with whatever puts you at your best. I've given tools throughout this book about being at your best, so please remember and practice them.

My point is not to bring shame, fear, and doubt to yourself internally by wishing that it didn't exist. After a while, in adulthood, the complaining gets tiresome. For example, a friend who wishes that they didn't have to work such long hours, or that her parents were more encouraging with her career choices, will be viewed as a complainer after a while. Regardless of what we wish for, to outwardly keep speaking on it without making a solid decision to do something about it, after a while, becomes complaining, and nobody likes a complainer.

This book intends to teach you coping strategies that will attract the people with the right energy; entertaining thoughts like this will only push them further away from you. Or worse, it will attract those that live in "complain mode" like you. The statement, "you are what you attract", is alive and real. If you find yourself thinking thoughts such as these, I encourage you to try to get a positive handle on it before you speak of it to others. In this case, it will not help you, but it will not harm you either. You will be at a neutral point in your life with it, in which you will not have to fight off bad friendships that you formed in the middle of that complaining, self-sulking phase.

When we face our fears and do just as much as someone with normal hearing does, then we are finding the beauty in it.

Find the beauty in it.

Two years ago, I joined a Young Adult Choir at my church. I had just joined a new church and was eager to join the singing ministry on stage, bringing joy and praise during church services. I had not even stopped once to think about all of the complications and confusion that I was bringing into my life. I did not consider that it would be yet another place requiring my full attention. Instead, I found the beauty in it. I dared to be the lesser hearing church choir sister that caught all of the words and lyrics. I pushed myself to read lips more during rehearsals. I planted an image of happiness with my smile, so if anyone "caught me" reading their lips to keep up, I could simply smile, and they would smile back. I alerted the ministry head that I would need her ears from time to time to make sure I heard all of the announcements and expectations. And guess what? It's been phenomenal. I stand on the stage alongside others, wearing a hearing aid and singing, and I smile because I did this.

When we face our fears and do just as much as someone with normal hearing does, then that is when we are finding the beauty in it. We are finding the joy in seeing ourselves while we thrive, regardless of it. Yet, these terrible thoughts of wishing it away will never allow you to be at your best and to experience life to the fullest because there will always be an intuitive feeling of wanting to hold back. I know that because I did it for years. Luckily for me, by adolescence, it was gone. That I am happy about, and I advise you that if you are past adolescence age and still engrossed in this awkward way of thinking, please begin to see the beauty in your hearing levels. What you accomplish while wearing hearing aids will bring you insurmountable joy. I promise you!

Habit #4: Stop overthinking it

The truth is that some decisions take longer than others, but not all decisions should take very long (which is when we overthink). Have you ever noticed that you are never able to have complete confidence in one decision with ease when you overthink? Most of the time, you probably won't even make a decision. You'll end up saying something like, "I will think about it later." If this is the case, then why not monitor yourself, realize when you are doing it and simply slow down your thoughts. Habit #4, overthinking can be defined as "obsessing about a situation continuously". It can also be tied to the act of fantasizing about different options more and more. It can be deemed as a "mental struggle", in my opinion.

Worry is never good for us in any way, shape, or form.

What can be helpful, I have learned, is to never underestimate the power of making quick decisions. I will talk a little more about making decisions more quickly soon, but for now, let's discuss why we should take charge of overthinking and why it matters for the lesser hearing. Worry is never good for us in any way, shape, or form. Worry is experienced when we overthink. There is simply no way around it. A lot of thoughts lead to worried thinking.

Even though you may eventually come to a confident decision and your decision may be very realistic, you still may worry about the decision that you made. I tell you, that is for the birds. Nothing should be this hard. And no decision should add to worry, the worry that we already deal with through acceptance of being of lesser hearing. What I mean is that, in our case, we come to deal with a situation as compounded worry; the worry of making a decision added to the worry of dealing with lesser hearing. Does that make sense?

Let me give you an example: Let's say that you are invited to happy hour with a co-worker. Everyone will be meeting up at Charlie's, which tend to showcase a band and have loud music that leads to high volume conversations. You have been to this particular venue before, so you are a bit hesitant to attend. All day, you wonder what you will tell your co-worker when she asks if you are up for attending. You may begin to worry about whether you have the time to attend, if you can find a sitter so quickly, if you will be able to make it home and back in time. It becomes compounded worry when you begin a separate reason of worry that sometimes may have to do with our hearing. For instance, you may start to worry whether Charlie's still showcases bands, whether it will be difficult to hear conversations, whether you will enjoy yourself, and the list goes on.

This is an excellent example of how overthinking is so very prevalent among our population. You may not see it as such, but the average person doesn't have to do this much worrying and doesn't have the means for having to overthink this much. That is why we need to understand the concept of overthinking and to derail it.

Aside from worry, overthinking tends to lead to anxiety attacks. Anxiety attacks happen as a result of stress. Simply put, when we stress and overthink, we just cannot get it together. This is just a habit that cannot be tolerated if we are trying to always be at our best. If you have this habit, I encourage you to work at changing it because holding it together is what successful people do. It is how you get to your victory and reach your full potential.

Isn't that victory a battle worth fighting for? Don't overthink it—overthinking causes us to daydream, waste time, and miss many blessings. Too many people become easily frustrated in the company of overthinkers. I will say it's one thing to overthink in your mind, but to let others know all of these endless thoughts, options, and ideas are just overwhelming. Your hearing is always going to be on your mind, but it has to be simplified, just like everything else in your life, or people will see that you are not handling it well.

Earlier, I mentioned the option of mastering the 'overthink bug' by becoming a quicker decision-maker. This would be such a significant breakthrough if you decided to give it a go. When we overthink, we tend to think that our initial thoughts or decisions are not good ones. As I said at the beginning of this chapter, some decisions do take longer than others, but not all decisions should take very long (which is when we overthink).

Master the "overthink bug" by making quicker decisions.

Master your overthinking by becoming a quicker decision-maker. Start with small decisions like what color peppers to use for dinner or what to wear to work, just the usual everyday things. Give yourself a week, and for all of the little things (and only the little things) that you do throughout the day, consider making a quicker decision. Of course, you will come to some bumps in the road, but every decision doesn't have to be perfect or lead to the perfect outcome. The thought is to simply begin to make quicker decisions and to do it with small decisions that will not hurt you as much. Think about it… would it really matter that you didn't wear your preferred jeans to the cocktail party when you walk in with confidence?

Yes, the inability to make quick decisions may have something to do with your confidence level, and the longer you take to pick out clothes in the morning. Okay, yes, some of us are picky dressers, but that is not who I am referring to. I am talking about the nervous dresser who cannot decide what to wear to church, who gets there, and ponders whether what she is wearing is the best she could have come up with. I will tell you something about picking out clothes, if you are still debating an outfit after you have arrived at an event, you may be on the overthinker side. Just think about it. When you arrive at an event, it's time to go with the flow and chill.

Habit #5: Tell them what you need, each and every time

Habit #5 is one that is all too familiar. In fact, it's one that we all have encountered too many times, I am sure. It's the one that has had the most impact and meaning, and when you eliminate this habit, you will bring yourself sheer joy and peace internally. That is the habit of telling people what you need, each and every time. Never let your inability to hear at normal levels dictate the respect that others should have for you.

Sometimes, we don't ask for what we need because we fear that we won't be answered with respect or that we will be judged. Well, two lessons should be learned in just that one sentence: 1) No one should disrespect you, and 2) Thou shalt not judge.

Simply ask for what you want.
Not sometimes, every time.

We are human, which means that in living our lives, we are going to come into circumstances and situations. The lesson is to never allow yourself to live less on account of someone else and their regards for you. They don't dictate how far your success in life will go, you do. I wish I could have told myself this years ago. Even into my early thirties, I was still not asking for what I needed. I was still fearful of how others would respond to me. I had birthed a child, excelled in the real estate world, and led a few ministries, but from time to time, I came into those situations when I still refused to ask for what I needed. I am admitting this because I want to show you how hard overcoming this habit can be for us.

> *People do not know the extent of your hearing loss; therefore, they don't know the extent of your suffering, so you have no choice but to tell them.*

It is, in fact, much easier to take the easier route and forego hearing what was said, but after a while, we get tired of missing things. We get tired of people laughing when we didn't hear the joke. However, if we had requested something to be repeated, we could have heard the joke and escaped the horrible feeling of being an outcast. There is no other way to do it, but to simply ask for what you want. Not sometimes, but every time.

Everyone has a few tricks up their sleeve, and of course, I have used them in the past, but at the end of the day, I was still not happy with not asking people for what I needed, each and every time. People do not know the extent of your hearing loss; therefore, they don't know the extent of your suffering, so you have no choice but to tell them. When people have conversations with you, and you have to ask them to repeat themselves, don't overthink a response. Listen to their repeated answer and move on. Most of the time, people aren't thinking about you, so I encourage you to get what you need—the very same way that they are not thinking about you when you rush through the door, soaked from the rain or crack your cell phone in the middle of a crowd.

In order to be more assured in asking for what you need, you have to understand the diversity of the modern world. We live in a world that has gotten to such tremendous growth in diversity that people don't stop to think about things out of the ordinary anymore. So, let's say that you have a conversation with someone on the train while on the way home from work, who "has never met someone with lesser hearing". During the discussion, if you have to ask them to repeat themselves continuously, then do it; have your conversation and keep it moving! Don't keep thinking about it all the way home. Once you have parted ways, then take your mind elsewhere. At the end of the workday, people can go to a coffee shop, attend a play, work on a website, attend a yoga class, and so on, so I doubt that they are thinking about the fact that they had to repeat a few things for you a couple of times.

That very person is probably now thinking about the errands she has to get done tonight, or what time her kids are arriving home. It may be her night to speak on her YouTube Channel, contribute to her blog, or work on the curriculum for a summer camp two weeks away. Refusing to ask for what we need keeps us in that stalled space. Too bad we cannot see for ourselves, that people go ahead and live without us, while we are sitting there dreading that we asked them to repeat themselves a few times. They aren't thinking about you. People have lives.

If they want to stop talking to you, then they will let you know. From my experience, I have not encountered people who outrightly say, "I refuse to repeat that for you". That is just something that you are not likely to run into. This world is so full of ways to connect that if people are bothered by your tendency to ask to repeat things, they probably will point you in the direction of an excellent site for hearing impaired, or even tell you there's a great app that is used by someone else that they know. That is the mode of operation of the world that we live in. People are astonished by apps and the many things that apps can do. Who knows, maybe you will meet someone who points you to the perfect app to help you bear through all of your days. That is the world we live in.

Habit #6: Stop using it as leverage

This last Habit #6 is probably familiar to some of us, but not all. It may have been used moderately, regularly, or not at all. It is the habit of playing the victim and reeling others in through guilt. It's not rocket science. Think about it, everyone takes a step back when you say, "I'm sorry, I didn't hear you because I have a hearing loss." Every cashier stops, and every phone customer service rep stops in their tracks to apologize. I can't say that I don't adore the ability to say something so eye-catching to others that make them think twice about what they just said to me.

We are in an age where customer service sucks. We get customer service representatives that want to give you minimal service. They will say something like, "Oh, all of the directions are on the box if you want to read them," instead of kindly guiding you through a device setup. In the world today, you truly get what you pay for, and that speaks volumes because most major corporations outsource customer service reps to other countries. This also means that we sometimes get representatives who are unfamiliar with the product and some who speak with strong accents.

So, picture this: They have asked you this same question again and again, and yet, you still cannot comprehend what they are asking due to their heavy accent. In turn, you shout back, "I have a hearing loss" and they rush to apologize, pleading that, in no way did they intend to disrespect you. Yes, that gives you leverage. You have taken back the power and now can get this unprofessional rep to listen to what you need. Oh yes, it gives you your power back, but it doesn't help the situation. What helps the situation is for you to go a step further and bring it to their attention that the accent is blocking your ability to understand them. It's a simple strategy, but I admit I have been guilty of choosing to obtain leverage by using my hearing loss. It is a habit that I cut short after a while, but I did give it a good run for a minute there.

People apologize so very quickly, and it's terrific, but if you have any sort of consciousness, you know that it wasn't an honest and fair conversational exchange. My point here is that this internally deteriorating habit has to stop. This habit doesn't only apply to the customer service rep; it appears in all areas of our lives. Sometimes, even as normal people, there are things that we don't want to do, but we cannot allow our hearing to be used as leverage, or an excuse not to do these things. In our relationships, friendships, clubs, on the job, etc., we have to be able to override the desire to use our lesser hearing as an excuse to fold.

In reality, it's not even about pleasing other people; it generally comes down to simply doing what is right. Is it right to shout louder to a friend that you didn't hear just because you became upset with the results of a conversation? Does it seem right to tell the cooperating parents that you cannot carpool the soccer team this week because you don't hear as well as others? No, it does not. Make a way.

This is the type of behavior that allows others to view us as disabled, and if you are looking for that, then be my guest and go right ahead. People will eventually come to see that you are not being truthful, and that will be a hard pill to swallow. So, yes, do what is right. If you didn't like the results of a conversation, but you know that you heard all of it, then ask the group if you can step aside to clear your head for a minute. If participating in the soccer carpool can get a bit overwhelming, ask another parent to ride along in the front seat to control the group while you drive.

My point is that in everything, show your capabilities and independence. Just remember that when we use our lesser hearing ability as leverage, we are causing doubt in others. We are allowing them to lift the eyebrow to us and consider that we may very well need more help than others. Is that really what we want? Since you are reading this book about coping strategies, I can probably rightfully assume that this would seem totally opposite of what you want. So, my advice is that you check your tendency to use your lesser hearing ability as leverage and don't do it again.

What a great chance to go over a few bad habits that we have in common and pinpoint how they hinder our progress. I hope that the examples given in this chapter have shown you just that. Good habits breed success, while bad habits breed failure. It's as simple as that. In our next chapter, we will discuss meaningful conversations and how to achieve them more in your life. It's so imperative that after you have finished reading this book, you have a plan for how to communicate better. The next chapter is going to show you just how to do this!

CHAPTER 8

The Three C's of Evolving Conversations... Change Your Ability to Have Meaningful Conversations!

> "Normal is nothing more than a cycle on a washing machine."
> —Whoopi Goldberg, Hearing Loss Actress

A WHILE AGO, I BEGAN to notice what was needed for me to have good conversations with others. These good quality conversations would help me to avoid spurious lashes against my self esteem. Real estate was a very "sociable" field. People regularly spoke about their investments, clients, new financing programs, and the last house they sold. I pretty much realized that if I didn't incorporate the Three C's into my conversations, then it is very likely that I would always be following the discussions and never dominating them. Leadership and domination enable us to be respected, and without it, we are constantly overlooked and underestimated.

The Three C's of Evolving Conversations

Now, I want to talk to you about the Three C's. They are *compassion*, *confidence*, and *chance*. Using this approach will help you begin to lead conversations better for the following reasons:

- You exercise compassion to the extent that you accept others.
- You are standing tall with your self-confidence.
- You are taking a chance to be heard.

Combining and acting on these Three C's should help you to nicely dominate conversations and be heard. This will improve your self-esteem and pushes you forward in a plunge to never settle for mediocrity. Let me explain.

Compassion

The first C is "the nice C." Compassion, as I introduced in Chapter 6 with my student, Eulus, is a great tool that can create reciprocity in conversations. What I mean is that compassion can create a greater flow of give-and-take through reciprocity. When people see your compassion during a conversation, they will want to keep you involved; they may even fill you in if you wear a look of "confusion" during a conversation. This happens because they have observed your compassion during exchanges, and in their eyes, may deem you worthy. On their own, they may come to a decision that you have listened to others, and therefore, have a right to be heard and hear everything, too.

*You can never go wrong
with having compassion for others.*

Showing compassion is a great social strategy that will increase the number of people who accept your presence. That's pretty much common sense when we think about it. A google search defines compassion as "sympathetic pity and concern for the suffering or misfortunes of others." (1). I would even take it a step further and not tie it down to "those who are suffering." Compassionate people are concerned for others at all times. They barely make things about themselves. So, yes, of course, people want more caring and sympathetic people to converse with. You can never go wrong with having compassion for others. A few examples may be assuring a groupmate who is going through hard times, that this, too, shall pass, or letting someone know they have a beautiful family while looking at pictures. The more you exercise these roles (with genuine words, of course), the more that people will return the sympathy and accept you into the conversation.

No, I'm not saying that you have to "kiss up" to anyone, but let›s not forget the dynamics of relationships here; there will probably be a time when you will need to call on someone to repeat something critical, such as, a professor that runs quickly through a lesson, or a staff meeting announcing significant changes in their HR policies. Try not to view this section as the one that "tells me that I need others so badly."

In fact, compassion is something that we should always work on to improve our lives. Start with a little compassion and build on that. Open a door for a lady or walk an older woman to her car, help an elderly man down the escalators, or teach a parent how to use an app that they want to learn for their child. Compassion should be a regular part of our lives, anyway, because in practicing it, we are actively acting and doing our part of giving. Then, when we are in need, there won't be any hesitancy for others to assist us with anything that we may need.

Decide to love yourself first.

Compassion doesn't just come to us on a whim. We have to decide emotionally to be compassionate to others. What does this mean for you? Well, in answering that, I am not sure because I have not lived your life. It may require a major life change of your thinking pattern. It may require you to love yourself more so that you can love others more. That is why I started this book with self-love and acceptance because I want you to decide to love yourself first, so that you have some chance of loving and accepting me (and others)—having compassion for me as an author and friend (and others) to take in what I (and they) am telling you. However, it may not be a major life change for you. You may already be a truly compassionate person. If that is the case, then great job with spreading the love around the universe; now, focus on channeling it into conversations and genuinely bonding with others.

In his book, *Seven Steps To Living at Your Full Potential*, Joel Osteen says that "one definition of compassion is simply feeling what other people feel, being concerned, and showing that you care." While writing this book, I read his book, and this chapter was a total eye-opener for me. I realized that I did not always show compassion like I wanted to, especially on my trying days. But, believe it or not, these are the days that it will empower you most.

> *We cannot expect to move through life happily when we are selfish and sulky. No, there is no reason that such behavior would be rewarded.*

These are the experiences that we need to see our potential outside of our physical abilities (which is sometimes lacking). Experiencing compassion will enlighten you to the beautiful person that you are. For instance, it may enable you to recall memories of earlier in the day, when you read a little girl a book in the library, and it caused you to say to yourself, "Hey, I'm a pretty nice person. I definitely deserve for others to go the extra mile for me." This is a trivial point in this section as well. You must know that you deserve the help of others; most of the time, this internal assurance that you deserve such will come by recalling when you have helped someone else. Make sense?

Anyway, in his book, Joel Osteen brought to my attention that compassion helps others who are in a struggle. He also said, "Everywhere you go these days, people are hurting. People are discouraged; many have broken dreams. They have made mistakes, and now their lives are in a mess. They need to feel God's compassion and His unconditional love." This is where we come in, helping when we can. We cannot expect to move through life happily when we are selfish and sulky. No, there is no reason that such behavior would be rewarded.

Confidence

The second C, which I refer to as "the big C," is confidence. Where would you be without your confidence? Where would I be without my confidence? I don't even want to imagine the day. My confidence took a while to build during my adolescent years, but once I got hold of a life so awesome, I was never letting go! Nope, there is no price you can pay to attain confidence, and there is no price that can be paid to take someone's confidence.

Take a second and think about your actual level of confidence. Is your confidence where it needs to be? If not, then why not? There are five primary senses of the body: touch, sight, hearing, smell, and taste. When one lacks, it's okay. Simply adjust by learning to maximize on another sense just to level it out. This trick has worked wonders for me. What do I mean by this? Use your eyes to increase your confidence.

Use your vision to pick up on vibes and happenings around you. Focus your eyes more on your surroundings and let them become your central point of protection.

Building inner confidence can truly have its climax when we are exposed to more trivial situations than ours.

Have you ever read *The Story of My Life* by Helen Keller? As I expressed to you throughout this book, reading is one of my best ways to escape. Imagine diving into a book, at twelve years old, about a woman who was both deaf and blind. Well, this book and its readings have stayed with me throughout my life to help me to see how blessed I truly am. In this book (written by a deaf/ blind author, which is phenomenal), Helen explains how maximizing her other three senses (smell, taste, and touch) helped her to better adjust to her living environment while being visually and hearing impaired.

Throughout her childhood, she was assisted by an in-house attendant, who helped her understand life (short of hearing and seeing) by taste, touch, and smell. For example, she spelled out words while touching Helen's hands, and Helen soon came to understand the concept of water by spelling out W-A-T-E-R in sign language, then feeling and tasting water.

For me, this book meant that my world was definitely adaptable. It was the perfect book to help me make sense of my life and begin thinking with more optimism. Optimism grows confidence. I was able to lighten up in my life and accept myself more. Really, if Helen Keller could become an author while both deaf and blind, then what was I waiting for? That is the same question that I pose to you today: "What are you waiting for?"

I encourage you to read this story if you have not already, especially if you are impaired in any fashion. Sometimes, building inner confidence can truly have its climax when exposed to more trivial situations than our own. For me, it created a rush of hope at just twelve years old. I know that many of you reading probably don't consider yourself to be as optimistic, subconsciously, as a twelve-year-old kid, the age where anything is possible. But, as I always say, knowledge is power.

The reality is that I knew less at twelve, and I get that; however, understanding the life of someone with a dual disability (such as Helen Keller) may just help you see how minor what having a hearing loss is because it is just that, minor. Another suggestion would be to google a few celebrities who have suffered from hearing loss, such as Bill Clinton, Whoopi Goldberg, or Halle Berry. This will help you to accept it as more commonplace, thereby, making it again minor, like it is!

In recalling your confidence level, you must also evaluate how you view this hearing loss. If it's considered a hindrance, realize that everything you try will be much harder than it is for the average person, simply because of your mindset. Let me say that again for the people in the back because it's so very important…

If your disability is mentally viewed as a hindrance to you, then everything you try will be much harder than it is for the average person, simply because of how you perceive it.

Confidence is matured by stroking, building and broadening our ego.

Okay, so you got that, right? Why do I say this? Because I have lived it—and you have as well—to see and know, by golly, that it is true! Just admit it already! Self-doubt makes the road longer. For instance, have you ever returned home from a long trip to a new place, but the ride back seemed so much shorter than the ride to the event? Well, that was self-doubt working in your mind the entire way there. When you're traveling a long, unfamiliar road with self-doubt, it honestly takes a lot longer to get there.

You're mentally worrying and doubting yourself the entire way. Think of it like an eager child on the way to an amusement park, saying to herself, "We're never going to get there!" Break the detrimental thought patterns of self-doubt as you embark on a positive journey. The concept of this book is to make your life easier, so let's try to "off" the view that your situation hinders your life in any way, shape, or form.

Confidence is matured by stroking, building, and broadening our ego, but this will require you to tone down the negative views of this hearing loss. Put these negative views on the back burner; let them burn out like a hot tea kettle forgotten on a back burner (a burner that's off, of course), and when you return, the water will be cool and rid of harmful, hot thoughts. Move on, and just let it merely be another part of your day.

Set your life up to succeed and do just that. This means to get organized, buy hearing aid batteries, service your hearing aids, research new device accessories, upgrade and renew your hearing aids, and keep it moving. A few years ago, my confidence shot through the roof when I took the chance and purchased a pretty plum color mold for my hearing aids. I was a bit skeptical at first because this pretty much gives people leeway to ask you, "Wow, how is that working out for you?" I didn't want to draw the "bigger crowd," but I am a very modern person as well. I love to watch technology thrive; besides, I did not miss a chance to pass up such pretty electronic devices.

In the moments leading to my decision to invest in colorful molds, I was tested. Yet today, I feel great because I know that I took a chance and passed those tests. I even met a few friendly people along with way. Wearing a colorful mold opened up doors to meeting others who wore hearing aids. It can be a great conversation starter, and then you can just take it from there. Amused people often stop me in the grocery store, restaurants, or while I'm at an outing and say, "Wow, I have wanted to try that, but I just don't know yet." They said the magic word… "yet." I feel like screaming at them, "What are you waiting for, just do it already!"

> *Stop thinking so far into what others think of you. Just like you have a hearing loss, they have their issues as well.*

I mean, we are in the day of beautiful iPhone cases, pretty purses, and lipstick to match. Why people continue to sport the bland natural colored hearing aids, I don't know. It's like choosing a boring caramel-colored Calvin Klein purse with a flashy hot Betsey Johnson purse sitting right on the same shelf. But to each his own. My increased circle of new faces has been amazing, and so has an increase in my confidence. Sometimes, I even refer to it as my bling-bling. It's pretty… the plum color deserves a cute name.

Moving further into confidence in conversations, remember that when we have conversations, our confidence creates magnetic energy. People are drawn to a confident conversationalist. It is not always her views or expertise that draws them in, but her audacity to speak out in front of the entire room is what creates the buzz. The same should be the case for you. Draw people into the conversation with your magnetic energy.

Stop thinking so far into what others think of you. Just like you have a disability, they have their issues as well. Being in very social networked fields, I have come to realize that people are simply not thinking about you, especially in very upscale event settings, such as company anniversary galas or investment happy hour settings. These people are more focused on how to win "their deal" than your little ten-second remark across the table.

No, you don't want to develop the habit of embarrassing yourself across the table, but you have to also be heard. With an increase in stating your perspective during meetings, your confidence will grow, and, over time, insecure feelings of hesitancy will subside. So, go ahead and ask your question at the next staff meeting. Stop pulling supervisors over after the meeting when they have already opened the floor to questions during the session. This is a relationship killer, and it works against your image. You never want to suggest that you require special attention unless it's necessary. In this case, just exercising a little confidence can get you over the bridge.

Confidence is the ability to dismiss the opinions of others and know that your thoughts and ideas matter. Many people are just not going to agree with you. That is life, but it doesn't mean that you cannot test your confidence; if they want to comment that your comment was unnecessary, remind them that they have their opinion and you have yours. That's confidence, and that would be another "episode aired" of being at your best!

Chance

The final C is "the optimistic C," chance. We don't see this particular word much in our world, but it's one of the most powerful words you will ever know and accomplish. Think about it… "to be given a chance," "to take a chance," or even "being blessed by chance," seem powerful and life changing. If I used any of these terms within a sentence, then more than likely, my life is changing and for the better.

Taking a chance is like a leap of faith.

At a dinner party that I gave last week, I had the luxury of cooking out, drinking some tequila, and chilling with a group of my closest friends. It was awesome. I had finally brought all of my closest friends together to converse and get to know each other. However, I looked across the table and noticed that my good friend, Kat, had not said much all evening. She had spoken with me earlier and assured me she was happy to be here. Still, during the group's entire "blown out of proportions, emotional conversation about society and its current-day changes," she had not commented on anything. I mean, she had not dropped two cents all night. She had not taken a chance. She had not been heard. She had not acknowledged her being within the conversation. I was fine with this, but then again, I was not, because this was a group of extremely close friends. I left it alone because I cannot make others act or speak. The evening continued, and it was awesome.

There is no great achievement in being comfortable.

My point is that she did not take a chance. She didn't give herself a chance. Taking a chance allows us to build confidence and to adjust to participating in the conversation. If you are never going to take a chance and add your two cents, the group will probably never come to you with questions because they will assume that you are, well, just not interested.

Taking a chance is like a leap of faith. At least people know that you are interested. I have a choir brother like this as well. Whenever we talk, it's always because I walk up to him and say hello. I am a friendly person, and I have been doing this with many of my sisters and brothers at church for years. A few weeks ago, I read a book while waiting for service to begin when he surprisingly tapped me and said, "Hello." I thought to myself, "Well, I'll be darned," and I told him that. It was a funny gesture, and hopefully, he has become comfortable with taking a chance and speaking.

My point is that we should not put that much thought into becoming comfortable enough to take a chance. There is no great achievement in being comfortable. Comfortable will not get you to the successful multi-million-dollar house in Silicon Valley. Comfortable will not get you to the raise or promotion that you so badly deserve. Comfortable will not get you the man or woman of your dreams. Everything in life happens by chance, and gosh darn it, sometimes you have to take the chance to create your chance! Sitting to the side, comfortable, will enable just that type of life, off to the side, unnoticed, never sought out. Is this really all that you want in life? In the words of Snoop Doggy Dog, in a song called "Drop it Like it's Hot," he says, "Take a second, think about it." And then goes, "Drop it like it's hot." Again, I am dying laughing, but at the same time, I am still singing the song in my mind. It's one of my favorites.

Whether you're greeting the CEO or saying your morning hello to the front desk receptionist, remember—it's your job, and your success requires that you take a chance. Some around you are not secure in all their decisions, but they are still taking the chance, which Kat and my choir brother were simply not doing.

Taking a chance is what puts us on the road to leadership. Jen Sincero, in her book, *You are a Badass: How to Stop Doubting Your Greatness and Start Living an Awesome Life* (great title by the way), she explains that sometimes there is no preparation, just jump in there and begin your greatness. She says, "to take the first right step, get out of your head and take action. You don't have to know exactly where it's going to take you. You just need to start with the one thing that feels right and keep following right-feeling things to see where they lead." I love authors, because again, as I sometimes say, I could not have said it better myself.

> *Get started, get cracking, and take your intuition along with you, and then you should be fine.*

We are also blessed with something so very powerful, called intuition. Intuition can be defined as the ability to understand something immediately, without the need for conscious reasoning. (2).

Pretty cool, right? This is something that Iyanla Vanzant (author and life coach) touches on a lot, both in her books and her television series, "Fix My Life." As she always starts by softly whispering to another the word "beloved," she always says, "I need for you to use your intuition." Truthfully, why does everything in your life always need a reason? Why can't we work with our intuition, that deep stomach gut that lets us know that something is right or wrong? Without intuition, life goes very slow, and opportunities are slow to come by because you simply wait too long to take a chance.

> *If you never take the chance, exercise confidence, and show compassion, then you will rarely be called upon.*

I am saying the same thing today that Iyanla Vanzant and Jen Sincero are both saying. Get started, get cracking, and take your intuition along with you, and then you should be fine. As a realtor (and this is an entirely true story), I had a client who missed so many opportunities for a lovely home because he just would not take a chance. He emailed me listings of beautiful houses, but always came up with an excuse not to meet up with me. He had excellent credit, great loan rates, money for a down payment, and an affordable plan, but he wouldn't take the chance. It was pretty sad. He would still be waiting when I called him back two years later, and then five years later. Get my point?

Taking this chance will also increase your chance of reciprocity, as discussed earlier in this chapter, the gift of exchange for mutual benefit. I know that in carrying a hearing loss, sometimes conversations don't go as we would like them to, and then we withdraw from the group. But with chance, if you have taken the chance and added your two cents, then maybe a friend or co-worker will reel you back into the conversation when they see that you are withdrawing. They may say, "Justine, did you hear what Annie just said? HR is thinking about giving everyone Christmas bonuses this year. Do you think that will happen?" And there you have it, your conversation continues, and you have been included and asked for your viewpoint.

I will say this. If you never take the chance, exercise confidence, and show compassion, then you will rarely be called upon. It's like doing double the work to be in conversations. We want people to call us back into the conversation. We shouldn't always have to rack our nerves to get back into the conversation, but if we refuse to take a chance, then people will assume that we don't want to be a part of it. If we don't talk with confidence, people will dismiss our opinions quickly. And if we don't show compassion, then we build brick walls during conversations.

So, trust that the program of the Three C's works together great. Trust that it is an effortless flow once you give it a good run a few times. In fact, it's a great way to measure how well you are improving your conversations. You could keep a journal and record your feelings or mishaps and watch yourself get better over time. My point is that to get started, you have to get started. Take a chance, infer your opinion, talk with confidence, and have compassion for others.

What I Have Learned in Conversations with Others

What I have learned in conversing with others is that, over time, we let our guards down more and more as we practice the Three C's. Pivoting points for you will occur because someone will eventually ask you outright about your hearing loss—although, in some cases, it very well may have already happened. At this time, it would be perfect for you to speak positively about it because they have taken an interest in it (and you) enough to ask you. We can gather two possible meanings of this. Number one, either they are interested in you and want to know better how they can adjust to your needs. This could be the beginning of compassionate, mediated relationships; or number two, they want your expertise to help a loved one with a hearing loss. Instances such as this place you in the role of a leader, where I want all of my fellow book readers to be.

We never know what people are going through.

This is something that I am so passionate about because, in our community, we simply don't have enough representation among leaders. Maybe there is more to your life than being someone's assistant. Perhaps your supervisor has a mother who has lost her hearing or a daughter with a severe hearing loss. Three C conversations can be your networking avenue to display genuine compassion for superiors and colleagues, if you view it and use it the right way, righteously.

You may be just the conversation a Pastor needs as he heads to the parking lot after service on Sunday, asking you about how you adjusted in your home environment and wants tips for moving his niece (who has a hearing loss) into his home. We never know what people are going through, and exercising the "nice" C, compassion, would put you right there as the focal point for others to get genuine care and help. Just something to think about as we look at the Three C's.

I want to prepare you for what is to come, as you step up and become more compassionate and caring, taking a chance in conversations and offering up your viewpoint more confidently. It's an accomplishment for us as individuals. To be sought out for our advice by others would be leadership growth within our population, because some with normal hearing levels who come upon this—dealing with a loved one who suffers—may be very overwhelmed; here we are, being the blessing to them in their hard times, as they have looked out for us. I'm so proud of you! Well, we are now ending our talk about change. You have the steps, strategies, and ideas. Hooray! Put them to use.

SECTION III

What You Can Expect

Lead Page III:
High Expectations Yield High Results

AS A READER, I am a firm believer in ending a book well. We can read an entire book, but if we cannot receive takeaways or gather meaningful perspectives, then book reading is just as pointless as watching television. I didn't plop you onto a couch in front of a TV screen. No, together, we have invested precious time in understanding a significant obstacle in our lives. If you are like me and never want to feel like you have wasted time, then, with any book, you will need to put everything together to make sense.

We're taking those coping strategies, and we're putting them to work. You have now heard the life experiences of another lesser hearing person (myself); my ability to adapt should show you that I have a pretty feasible plan. We should now be more aware of our tendencies as lesser hearing; we have also identified some things that we need to change. So, now you may ask, "Okay, Dominique, I have done all of these things. What can I expect?" My answer is, expect an awakening that reaps abundance. In more layman terms, you're all set.

Yes, once you get through Chapter 9 when you start to build your inner circle, and Chapter 10 when you will understand this awakening, then I promise that you will begin to live life with expectations and void of excuses. Read on...

CHAPTER 9

Build Your New Inner Circle... Expect Relationships to Blossom from Here on Out!

> *"Don't take yourself too seriously. Know when to laugh at yourself and find a way to laugh at obstacles that inevitably present themselves."*
> —Halle Berry, Hearing Disabled Actress

Ace Your Test

There will be times when you will be tested in your walk of life, and there are tests of your intelligence, your faith, your commitment, your patience, your compassion, etc. However, when you experience these tests, understand that they are a part of life. It helps us to develop strength and drive. Life and its tests increase our livelihood; when we ace them successfully, we are better set for whatever comes our way. We are then granted the possibility of reaching our maximum potential.

There is such a dire and low amount of strength in a life that has not been tested. For instance, let's say that you have an overly sensitive friend who has not been tested in her walk of life much. She has not learned to stop taking things too personally, and as a result, she is overly sensitive to everything around her. She can be overly sensitive to the smallest things: she's sensitive to a cashier line with just two people ahead of her, she's sensitive because she has to cook breakfast every morning, or she's even sensitive about too many people sitting at her table for lunch. This is the trait of a person that has not been able to explore life's full potential since she has not yet "tested" or moved past her overly sensitive way of living. It's quite similar to a blood clot deep down in her arteries, blocking the blood for survival; it is a massive blockage in her life.

Good friends increase your internal strength.

So, how do we ace these "tests" of life, and become better people? How do we analyze to see that we may be over-sensitive, over-dramatic, or over-emotional? Let's face it, these are all symptoms of weaknesses and low amount of internal strength. Most of the time in our lives, a good friend is pushing and encouraging us through the storms, shuffling us and probing us forward across the finish line.

Good friends increase your internal strength. But first, it does take your own will to open up to them, allowing them to be a good friend to you. If you are among peers who don't push you forth to test your strengths and challenge your weaknesses, those peers aren't doing their jobs; perhaps you need better peers. Friends and family know us sometimes better than we know ourselves and, that is what this chapter is all about: YOUR CIRCLE.

What is a circle?

I use the term 'circle' because I often used it in the business world. It can be called a "sphere of influence" or a "network." However, what I am talking about here is using it for personal growth. Friends come from all walks of life, but who you allow into your personal space will determine your potential in every area of your life. So, it all comes together in the end. If you're an A+ friend, then more than likely, you are able to build great relationships with coworkers and colleagues. Make sense? Yep! So, let's now begin to focus on our circle. Circles are the people that surround you. They can be childhood friends, cousins, neighbors, soccer coaches, team members, ministry sisters and brothers, coffee buddies, college friends, and the list goes on. Anyone in your life can be a part of your circle, but here are a few questions to ponder:

- Do you really want to allow everyone to be a part of it?
- Are you willing and able to obligate yourself to that many people?
- Is your time able to be stretched that far?

- What type of people do you want your circle to be made of?
- What kind of energy do you want within your circle?
- Who is good or bad for your circle?

We live in a world where we all need each other.

Just a few questions to get your interest bubbling about this great circle for now, but understand that your circle, over time, will grow to be cherished for its sprinkles of sunshine and positivity, among many other things. Now, your question may very well be: What does this circle have to do with my life's progress and being one that hears at lower levels? And that answer is *everything* because your internal strength is everything! How you treat those in your circle and how that is reciprocated is your entire world and existence.

Yes, it's truth that our actions are our own. We eat, breathe, and sleep all on our own; however, we don't reach new heights and potentials alone. Many well-established and famous folks would vouch for this as a known fact. We live in a world where we all need each other. That is true. However, doing it alone brings with it a ton of unnecessary struggle.

Look for positivity outside of yourself.

When we set out to accomplish mighty things all on our own, let's keep in mind that our minds are half the battle. Our mind hesitates; it second guesses. Until you have reached a point of

TOTAL self-cleansing and FULL spiritual soundness—which is not very likely, as these traits are known to continuously grow and evolve—then, yes. . . we do need the words and encouragement of our circle to "block out the mess" in our minds. I'm not saying to give others the power over your mind; I'm saying to look for positivity outside of yourself. With a supportive circle of friends, you will get it.

The Law of Attraction does exist.

Years of highs and lows have taught me that my walk was much harder when all of my encouragement was internal and came from self-evolved behaviors. This is life, and there will just be days that you cannot find the drive to lift yourself. No millionaire has become a millionaire alone; if you ever meet one that tells you such, then you should, in a heartbeat, hit the ground running in the opposite direction because they are lying through their teeth, so they clearly don't have your best interest at heart.

Okay, I'm joking right now, but I'm sternly serious in what I am conveying as well. Every single millionaire has his or her set circle. They know that each member of the circle is there for a particular reason (or reasons), and they call on them in those times of need. Yes, my walk has always been careful and disciplined, but I have passed through a period in my life that has taught me to never do it alone. Lord, I'm shouting to the holy hills, "I don't need that lesson again." When we don't pass these lessons the first time, we will have to return to these lessons in life again. No, sir. . . not doing it. I want my life to be about progress, and you should want the same.

Step it up a notch and watch the law of attraction work in your favor.

Don't make yourself live these lessons over and over. This will only spring you into a life of repeated circles of blissful and endless self-doubt and self-induced traumas. I need you to get this lesson. There is a lesson in life of overcoming the tendency to struggle with self-doubt and hesitancy. There is also a lesson of procrastinating and the refusal to just *get started*! These two lessons, alone, create great internal struggle and the tendency to overthink. Those are already two stressful factors. When we commit to a circle, open ourselves up to those we can trust, and refuse to do things alone, the law of attraction can be a blessing. When we use our circle and help others, the law of attraction sees us prioritizing others' needs; it sees us humbling ourselves and taking our minds off of ourselves. I like to think of it as a pretty green turtle surrounded by other turtles, and this turtle is breaking out of a selfish shell; when this happens, the law of attraction sends others to help it! Cool, right?

Don't get me wrong… my understanding of turtles is that they are loners and want to be left alone. Turtles don't need to be cuddled or even given attention. Actually, it's a boring lifestyle, I might add; however, that makes my point even more valid. Boring lives don't lead to major accomplishments. Boring lives don't help other people. Boring and alone doesn't provide the environment to help others. Get it? We are not animals—we are humans who need interaction, love, and acceptance from others. Therefore, why not step it up a notch and engage your circle with ways to help them, then watch the law of attraction work in your favor.

Let me share a situation with you. A while ago, I had a friend who was starting her job search during a season when I was also hopping back into the job market, so along with her trustworthiness, she was an ideal friend for my circle at the time. We often spoke of the same issues, and we encouraged each other. One of her strengths was that she had always had such good, energetic professional conversations with many people about work ethics, integrity, customer service, and so many other issues. She was also very kind.

On this particular morning, I simply could not muster up the drive to start any job search tasks as I had planned to. I dragged myself out of bed, dragged myself to the kitchen for coffee, then to my office to get in front of my computer. I just sat there—simply stuck and hopeless. It just was not a good day in my book. I decided to step away from my laptop for a while and place a call to her, and boy was I glad I did! She was filled with great energy and enthusiasm. . . energy that I was void of, riddled with shame and sorrow. Apparently, her morning had gone differently than mine, so she had so much that she wanted to share with me. As much as I tried to hold on to my crabby dwelling spirit with every fiber of my being, her sense of genuine caring and sharing refused to let my heart dismiss her words. She was contagious. Her energy had won me over.

She told me about a great interview packet that she had received from a colleague and how she was tailoring it to fit her upcoming interview. After ten minutes of her ecstatic energy, I realized that I was experiencing a moment that could be very beneficial to me. What was I doing? Didn't I need this, too? I shot a quick thought to my brain and said, "Dominique, get out of your feelings... uhh!" I had picked up the phone, dialed her number, and indirectly caused my prayers to be answered by placing my needs aside and calling to see how she was doing.

I had come out of my selfish shell and put her needs first; as a result, I was about to be blessed tremendously by merely being there for a friend. Yet in my heart, my intention was not to walk away with such a good wealth of information. This packet and this situation, along with her sharing, allowed me to find a moment of hope and positivity for myself in the middle of a very dreadful morning; with that, my self-loathing attitude was out the door. I had reached out and used someone in my circle at a time when I needed help; I forfeited the need to do it all alone and was blessed tenfold!

Accept the accomplishments of others...

When you start to see the power of your inner circle, you will begin to accept others' accomplishments (even in the middle of your self-pity) as a blessing to you. Let me re-emphasize this by stating it again: When you accept what others accomplish in your time of pity, it will always be a blessing to you, as well. That's just the law of attraction. When people are in their happy time, they are at the height of their giving stage. So, if you parade them on, then true friends will want you to get some happiness from it.

Be the bigger person with the right heart.

No, I cannot guarantee you a tangible blessing every time you get out of your feelings, but I can guarantee you some peace soon—if you get over yourself and start to be happy in the midst of others celebrating their success. What is the old fashion phrase that many people used to cling to? Oh yeah, "be the bigger person." Well, yes, be the bigger person with the right heart and start bringing positivity, too. Get out of your feelings and learn to be happy for others. With this, I promise you your time is coming. I am walking proof of this.

The secret to getting through these difficult moments is believing that the energy you put out there, you are sure to receive back. This should end that everlasting internal struggle within all of us to have that simpler life, a life without dreadful hearing aids, a life void of having to ask people to repeat themselves, and a life filled with self-assurance. Your life is your own, and you must take steps to believe and receive this and, in these moments, pay close attention to how you're actually feeling.

Your energy has to be pure, genuine, and authentic, and in these moments, if you begin to feel any inkling of jealousy, then release these hater emotions and strive to see the good in that person and why they deserve it. I have a slogan that I use a lot, both in social media as hashtags and verbally as a cue to stop hating. I say, "Don't hate, congratulate!" Yes, get out of your feelings and stop blocking other people's moments. This will help you to curb your desire to want to live the life of others. It will make you appear to be more graceful and loyal to others, and people will be drawn to you like a moth to a flame!

Attract the right people

While building your inner circle, you want to be sure to attract the right people. I am jumping with glee and overjoyed to convey to you that you have total and complete power over who you attract! Every person that you attract into your life, you are unintentionally attracting them. What people don't often realize is that people are attracted to you through body language, and the images that are held in your mind are often reflected through this body language.

Envision good things for yourself
and speak them into existence.

Years ago, I read a great book called *Secrets of the Millionaire Mind*. This book gave me so much new drive to think, desire, and live like a millionaire. I realized that my current way of thinking was wrong and affecting my financial prosperity and that it had to be changed. I learned that I had to envision good things for myself and speak them into existence. I had to speak "becoming the millionaire" and "make blessings that would bless others" into existence. I was determined to apply what I was learning from this book so that I could also become a millionaire.

The energy that I received from people and the friends that I made was awesome. It was as if a lightbulb had gone off in my head and caused me to venture into life as a whole new person. My personality was on point, I was sharp and graceful, and people could see and feel it. All of them were drawn to this rare energy of positivity that I exerted. I knew this because they spoke on it and were delighted by it.

A few people said, "Wow, I've gotta be more positive like you." This showed me that I was headed in the right direction. As I began to ponder the reactions I received from people, I started to realize that the optimist was more like the person that I wanted to be.

No, I didn't rain on the parade of others before, but I didn't dance along with them to the band's tune in the parade, either. Previously, it was as if I simply stood to the side and watched the parade go by with a mediocre feeling. Now, I had learned to dance alongside friends in their accomplishments to the beat of the drum, and that drew the crowd; amid the crowd, I formed awesome friends.

Here's an example I am sure you will love, as you more than likely have done this before. Have you ever talked with someone who continuously smiled and then found yourself smiling? When people say smiling is contagious, I assure you, it really is, people! As infectious as yawning, I might add. It's tough to stare with a deep 'mug' into the face of someone who is constantly smiling. It's an unbreakable thing! Whew! I love it!

My point is that, for me, it was the year of broadening my inner circle to include more people who were attracted to me because of this positive energy that I was placing into the earth. If they found it charming, then who knows how many friends I could make! What I came to see is that I was attracting the right people because of who I was becoming. Therefore, I could not go back to being the person that I was before because they would begin to ask, "When did you become so cynical?" It was a challenge worth following through on because I appreciated what was happening in my life. More than anything, I appreciated who was coming into my life. I mean, they were positive, optimistic people who had goals just as I did. They were envisioning their millionaire futures, too, and this was awesome energy to give and receive on both ends.

The law of attraction is fantastic, but like everything, there is a good and bad side. The opposing negative side reaps chaos and is usually expressed using insults and sarcasm. I will sum it up quickly and easily for you; very simple, you attract what you put out there. Throw an insult or joke out there, and you will get one back soon, maybe even more rapidly than you think. Insults and jokes are hurtful and painful, and believe it or not, they hurt, and pain will be returned to you. Is life not hard enough yet that you need to produce other situations that bring you pain? Kinda defeats the purpose of living, right? Remember, these situations only bring this pain because you choose to take part in giving it. Correct?

Let me share a story with you. I had a friend who I met in a local library one day, becoming friends. He often complained of his job, and he passionately felt that he was not paid enough or taken seriously by his supervisor. I talked with him about it and shared with him that, most of the time, it's about how we present ourselves that determines how others treat us. In his refusal to accept my logic and prove to me that he just had stubborn supervisors, that he worked for a bad company, he invited me to an anniversary gala sponsored by his company. According to him, he wanted me to have a first-hand glimpse of what he was talking about.

At the event we had dinner, we conversed and laughed with colleagues; he introduced me to his superiors and coworkers, all the while being respectful, but that didn't last long. As soon as dinner was over, and the awards were presented, he tossed drinks with the work crew and spoke his mind freely. It was awful. He was throwing insulting jokes and mocking his boss—outrightly complaining about how his boss ran the shift. It was such a disgrace to witness. His coworkers were glimpsing at each other with signs of disbelief. Jaws were dropping all around the room. It was just terrible. I could sense the supervisor's embarrassment, and returned to my seat, dodging conversations with him for the rest of the night.

After the occasion, I talked with my friend a few days later. Oh, I was ready to let him have it! How could he be so immature and embarrass his boss so badly? I asked him how he expected to ever get a raise at this job with all the mockery he throws around. He said, "It's fine, they know me there. I make jokes all day at work; they're used to me." I was horrified. I had known him to be a bit of a playful jokester sometimes, but for him to not realize how it affected his job was simply a shame.

I then asked him what he thought of my energy at the gala. "Oh, I love your energy, Dominique. You're sweet, everyone was happy to meet you, and they asked to have you back next year. I know you're not going to do that kind of stuff to people," he replied. Really? I was not even flattered by him being smitten with my sweetness. I was more disgusted that he had contradicted himself. It was as if he was telling me indirectly how he felt about himself.

> *We must look inside ourselves and understand why we don't prioritize treating others well.*

When we do "that kind of stuff" to people without accountability, then we have to look inside ourselves to understand why we don't prioritize treating others well. Do we take time to think before we speak? Do we work to positively control our environment and how others receive us? Is this just behavior we walk upon, or are we aiding these terrible responses along?

They heard you the first time.

All of these questions are the questions to ask ourselves if we want a better circle. Within a supportive circle, you feel desired, you want to treat people right, and you see the respect that people have for you through their actions. If you're still not convinced, then here is something to think about when building your circle. It's pretty simple: People heard you the first time! Hello! That's one of the significant truths to life that will help you to take a step further to decide who to cherish and spend time with.

Good friendships flow, people are there for you, and you don't have to repeatedly ask them to do things. People who care, heard you the first time, and if you're in their heart, then your needs will matter to them enough not to repeat it. It's just that simple. I have tried my hardest to get around this for years, and I'm hollering it to the sky, "It ain't happening, they heard you the first time!" I can't begin to convey the amount of many wasted hours of unworthy people you will encounter if you don't understand and apply this to your circle.

So, how do you apply it? It's easy as pie! You simply watch people and their responses to you. If someone didn't show up at your event, call you back, or missed your birthday—when you told them your birthday was important to you—please take that as a sign. What we are not capable of doing is reading the mind of others, so instead, follow your gut. Yes, that feeling that "something about this doesn't feel right" is powerful, so don't ignore it! Also, please, pretty please, don't forget the experiences you've had.

Don't forget how it felt to be stood up, or how you felt when you didn't receive the birthday call, because if you choose to ignore it, then I promise that it will happen again. People show you how much you mean to them, so don't be so quick to dismiss what they put you through. If they are worth it, then approach them, and if they refuse to regard your feelings or prioritize this, move on!

Let go of the schoolyard friends. Yes, remember the mean little girl on the playground who always made recess worst for you? Everyone knows a schoolyard child like that. Well, it was Shawntay for me, when I was in the fourth grade in elementary school. Shawntay rolled her eyes at me continuously and was always starting stuff or talking about me to my friends. For some reason, she just didn't like me. She would act out, I would run and tell a recess teacher, and the teacher would "mend the friendship." My twin sister put out this fire for me (bless her heart), by approaching Shawntay after school one day.

Dominese, my twin sister, saw me crying one afternoon at dismissal while getting my bookbag, and she asked what was wrong. I told her, "Shawntay said she's gonna beat me up after school." Dominese was not having that. Like I said before, she was my protector. She marched me out to the front yard at dismissal, right up to Shawntay. She said, "Did you tell my sister you would beat her up? Because I will beat you up." Shawntay was scared because Dominese wasn't in our class; she barely knew her or even knew that I had a twin sister. Shawntay ran away quickly and went home. She returned to school; we got along for a few days, and then she reverted to her same mean ways. I will never forget that time in my life.

Now, in this adult life, I say to hell with Shawntays. Who has time for the schoolyard drama during adulthood like this?

And all people want to do is "fake" mend friendships with their empty apologies, just like the recess teacher did, only to have them fall apart again! Empty apologies often begin with "I'm sorry if ____." Enough said. Recognize it. Cut them out and move on.

Some people just aren't cut out to be friends...

Friendships that fall apart again, now, that's another sure sign of bad inner circle friends: Continuous conflicts with the same friends. Some people just aren't cut out to be our friends. I personally believe in the slogan that friends are meant for "a reason, a season, or a lifetime." I can remember the friends that I allowed back into my life, even when it was pretty darn evident that our time was up, only to live through the chaos and disappointment again.

Life is about peace, and some people just aren't worth it.

Even if it's happening with more than one friend, give yourself the benefit of the doubt that it's not you, but simply the process of clearing your inner circle. I mean, maybe you just have a few rug rats you need to rid your circle of. Perhaps it's your entire circle even. In case you have not learned by now, life is about peace, and some people just aren't worth it. You forgive them, and they turn back around and shoot you in the foot again. Except, it's even more painful this time because you accepted them back into your life, along with their flaws, the first, second, and third time. This is not a relationship that exhibits a flow if you have to keep coming and going and mending and fixing. Call it a day and move on! You would do better using this time to love and work on yourself.

Let me ask you something. How many argumentative conversations have you had when you actually changed someone's mind? I probably can count them on one hand; and really, I probably will not even need that one. The truth is, people don't change because of us or because of a conversation. They don't change over a few conversations. They change because of life's happenings or because they simply realized a life-changing need within themselves to fix something. I refuse to partake in argumentative exchanges. I choose to believe that people who argue their points haven't realized for themselves how powerless they are to change others.

On the other hand, most of the time, when people seek out your advice, they more than likely have situated themselves to take in what you will say to them. If they ask me for my opinion, then sure I can spare you a few minutes and my two cents, but other than that, no thank you. Even after listening to you, they will probably still want to give it some thought. So really, what is the likelihood of changing people's minds in a heated argument? Slim to none, my friend. Maybe, it's just me, but I just don't have the time to sit and disagree, and then we've wasted thirty minutes. No, I could have met someone who gave me some insight in that thirty minutes to get a few steps closer to becoming a millionaire.

Sorry, not sorry. Life is about maturity, and those who are not committed to their words and bonded to their actions are doomed, in my opinion. Nope, not getting my time. I would not dare. Besides, we are all adults here; if I have to tell you twice, you get the boot. Don't get me wrong, I have a lot of patience for others, but I use my spirit of discernment too. I mean, yes, people sometimes mess up, but just be very careful of people and their intentions. The law of attraction asks that we place kindness into the earth, but everyone is not mature enough to give it back. Do you understand where I'm going with this?

Everyone doesn't deserve the boot.

Okay, so I will say that everyone doesn't always deserve the boot. For some, if you don't choose to shift your foot upwind and give them the boot, then you must know, for sure, without a doubt, that their love is real and genuine. My younger sister, Quintina, has had a couple of slip-ups with me in our lifetime, but she is also the perfect example of pure love. She is a CEO girl boss with a super busy schedule. She creates so much inspiration in me and is a total asset to my circle. But some people do have good intentions. If she misses a momentous occasion, then she will be sincerely apologetic about it; therefore, I never make a big deal about it because I know her obligations, lifestyle, and heart.

At the end of the day, actions speak louder than words.

She says things like, "Oh my goodness, Sis, did I miss that?" But she genuinely means it. Even if she misses an occasion here or there, her outnumbered efforts in my life repeatedly show me that she cares. Quintina is glorious at repeating things for me. Never have I felt an inkling of hesitancy to ask her, "What did they say?" She will even add a sweet laugh in there to show you it's okay to ask. Yes, nobody is perfect, but this is my sister, whom I've known my entire life. Many other people I would dare to be this lenient and trustworthy with these matters, and my foot would be quickly shifted upwind because, at the end of the day, actions are louder than words.

Let's get to work

Now, since we have covered the true essence of good friends and terrible foes, let's get back to what this chapter is about—this wonderful inner circle you're going to create. We are going to begin making our new and exciting fabulous, yet genuine, connections as we build this tool of brilliance. Oh yes, it's going to be sprinkled with great wonders like respect, power, and boundaries. Respect in our circle will allow others to engage with us in respectful ways. Respect will also attract the right people when we convey our disability confidence and allow you to grow by hearing others' views, in exchange for having yours heard.

Power in our circle enables us to be happy for others, even when we are not at a time that we are shining in our own lives. It springs forth courage within to celebrate for others. I want to share just how powerful this can be in a circle when these dynamics are multiplied. Finally, setting boundaries with others will allow you to share what you expect from others in your circle. Yes, boundaries will help you to avoid building relationships with wishy-washy people. The people who say things like, "Well, you never told me that." And yes, boundaries will also allow you to voice your needs and avoid getting hit with surprises along the way. I want to elaborate, section by section, on all of this coming up!

Respect in your circle

Have you ever stopped and come to terms with your hearing loss? When you have come to terms with it, it will show in your walk, talk, and body language. It will spring forth exuberant energy in you, and that my friend, will attract peaceful people your way. That is, interactions blossom into beautiful, mutually fulfilling friendships. If you want respectful relationships, then people must see you as confident, instead of burdensome. When people feel that a relationship with you may cause a burden on them, they will reject invitations to get to know you. It makes perfect sense, and it doesn't have to be rocket science.

Think of it this way, how you convey it, they will receive it. If it is viewed as a burden to you, then it will be a burden to them, and burdensome people never receive much respect. Nope, respect is earned through integrity. In other words, "Watch me converse with integrity; that will make you wish I were talking to you." Oh my God, I'm killing myself here. I sound like a man on a date, trying to pick up a woman. But anyway, my point is that what I'm asking you to do takes confidence, which means coming to terms with your hearing loss. You must be confident and driven, like everyone in your circle, or I promise that you will leave, or withdraw from the circle, a perfectly good circle that you created. So, if you need to revisit earlier chapters about confidence builders, then I encourage you to do that.

Flock upon me

It's such an incredible achievement to have others flock to you, or should I say, be drawn to you and your energy. So, here's the question: Are you a flocker, or do others flock upon you? Do you run to coworkers as they enter a room, or do people seek you out? This all comes down to something that many people don't give ample attention to—meaningful conversations. This is especially impressive when practiced by the lesser hearing. People are sometimes so busy staring at your hearing aid that they can't follow the conversation, and the minute you sweep the group off their feet, they are left wondering how you did it.

Say that it's the company's Christmas party, and your coworker walks into the room with his/her spouse. Do you think that they want to sit with someone with meaningless conversations? Well, okay, on the one hand, we have those attendees who only come for the food, the drinks, and to cut the rug! However, if you're genuinely trying to learn the art of making the most of the occasion and building your circle while you're at it, these occasions are your times to connect. So, let me ask you again, are you the flocker, or are you flocked upon? And I will just say, for the record, that the latter is better in case you're not following.

> *It's okay to be the flocker for a while,*
> *but the goal is to become flocked upon.*

Have you familiarized yourself with how to have meaningful conversations and how to avoid having meaningless conversations? Are you aware that meaningless conversations waste your time and the time of others as well? The type of conversation that is valuable and full of meaning builds respect and allows you to embrace those who are respecting you.

Why are we talking about this? Well, mainly because you're trying to build a better circle of friends. You're trying to take your life to the next level and meet more influential people. As you continue to build your confidence for occasions and events, it's okay to be a flocker for a while as you learn the tricks of the trade, but the goal is to eventually become flocked upon. Think about how great that would be for people to say, "Oh, here she comes now, the woman of the hour," as they welcomed you over. Yes, it would be exciting and mind-blowing, but first, we've got to work on having more meaningful conversations.

Find your niche; be able to talk passionately about it, love it, and share it.

First, you must find your niche, talk passionately about it, love it, and share it. What do you talk about with ease? What do people come to you for advice about? Many times, people ask me about my optimistic view on life and how I juggle so many obstacles. Or, they may ask me how to get started on an idea that they have been lingering on since forever. Maybe you are great at bargains and coupon collection. Maybe you have done extensive research on world theology. Take a few weeks and observe what people tend to talk with you about.

Learn to sell your perspective.

What you must begin to look for is what will build more meaningful conversations. Make a list, if you would, and just write down five things that you feel people tend to question you about and then begin to read more about them to be ready for the next office party, happy hour or seminar; watch people stand around in amazement as you sell your perspective. That's what life is about, having perspective. I mean, how much are we living if we have not learned to form opinions and back them up with facts and research.

My niche is something that drew me to writing this book. From high school to college to the workplace, all of my friends in all walks of my life have always told me that I have so much enthusiasm, although I suffer from a hearing loss. It was a bit offensive at first, but when I started to read and understand what others suffering from hearing loss go through, I began to understand what my friends had been subjected to with others who faced the same issues.

My blessing was that I was raised in a family of the lesser hearing. We make jokes about it, and we readily sympathize with each other; it's something that is accepted across the board over many generations. However, as I began to validate my feelings on the lesser hearing's thoughts and views, I learned that I still had a lot to learn. So, I started to fully understand what was happening in my world, not just the world around me. Then I could get more people to listen to me and accept my opinions and experiences because my words weren't covered in selfish "this is my life" talk, but conveyed with facts, assurance, and empathy.

There is no room for questioning yourself or uncertainty when it comes to introducing yourself.

Here's a thought—and a true one indeed: every respected person in a circle of people has a specialty, and this specialty that we all possess is how people introduce you into a group. For instance, a person in a group might say, "This is Darren, he runs a few nonprofit children's programs in the city," or "This is Denise, she has worked with a lot of condo builders in the area." The question now becomes, how do people know you? How do people introduce you? This may be a bit of a challenge for you, indeed, if you've developed self-doubt patterns in your career or your personal life. Yes, in order to present yourself well, you must have come to terms with your life and show full acceptance of yourself. So, let's get it together, people!

There is no room for questioning yourself or uncertainty when it comes to introducing yourself. Why? Well, because people present you to others in the same way that you introduce yourself. Of course, it's not always verbatim, but I promise they will adopt the same energy that you use if you were to introduce yourself. Have you ever noticed this? Mike says, "Hey, everyone, I'm Mike. I'm just a power plant operator, and I work long night shifts." With his chosen words, he has created negative energy in the group. I can promise that when Kim walks over, Ed will say, "Hey Kim, this is Mike, he's just a power plant operator who works long night shifts," and then the rest of the party will regard you as an unhappy night-shift worker. The word "just" has to be eliminated from your vocabulary if you truly want genuine acceptance from others. It's as strong as the words "I'm sorry" when there are many other ways to apologize. My point is that certain words simply devalue you. It's as simple as that.

However, let's try this a different way. "Good day, everyone. My name is Mike. I work for Exelon Energy as a power plant operator. We're on the brink of making wonderful innovative changes, and the company is growing; it's an excellent opportunity for me." Imagine being shared around the group on your behalf. Yes, you have everyone thinking, "absolutely, energy matters." Sometimes, people are yearning for just one positive person in the entire group; this will get you the respect and admiration needed to draw them into your circle.

People gravitate to positive, confident energy.

A year ago, I attended a three-day event sponsored by a major data distribution company called DataStax, Inc. The program attendees were mostly computer engineers. The interaction level was low and dull as we began the start-up for the boot camp. I kid you not; it was so boring that when the emcee did fifteen physical push-ups on the stage as the initial introduction, this group of people barely laughed. Sucks, right? Well, it's times such as these that create your opportunity to shine. I was attending as a newbie to the data management field, totally optimistic, and ready to begin boot camp for building a power tower database. I parked my laptop in the very front row, took a seat up front, and proactively joined in the discussions and dialogue.

> *There is simply not enough positive energy to go around, so bring it!*

After the keynote address, the emcee said, "And now, we're going to have our icebreaker session, but first, I want to begin with this young lady right here in the front," he swung his microphone around to me! I was ecstatic, but I'm a go-getter, so it was the perfect opportunity for me to get my limelight! I said, "Yep, I'm from the area, so it's just like being at home; this is the cookout in the backyard for me. I'm new to databases but super excited to be here."

This intro overwhelmingly turned the energy of the event around, and throughout the event, every presenter, teacher, vendor, was calling on me. I even met the CEO, a beautiful woman who said, "Thanks for the intro, that is exactly the energy that we're looking for." People gravitate to positive, confident energy. Let me say that again, *people gravitate to positive, confident energy*. Plainly put, there is simply not enough to go around, and if you bring it, you will earn your respect!

Question: have you ever noticed how sad, sullen people tend to sit alone, but a crowd of people will gravitate towards one excited person? No, I'm not saying you have to be Michael Jackson, but claiming yourself as the 'man in the mirror' who's about changing the world wouldn't hurt. It's not a popularity thing; it's a man on a mission thing. Every goal that you announce should address how it helps others. People gravitate to people who care. They want to know your why, and this takes opening up and also being positive. You do have to be careful with this, though.

You don't want to bore people about raising reading literacy levels or recent tax laws. Just give them a little and gracefully begin to listen to them. If they want more information about you and your plans, they will usually ask a follow-up question. That's how you have a good conversation, and that is a reciprocated respectful conversation; that's mastering respect and growing your circle. Common signs that people lack respect for you include side-eye glances, minimal conversation, one-word answers, mocking, cliques formed, hurried answers, and outright discouragement from hearing your opinion. Sometimes, you will see this. Accept that after a few occurrences, this is probably not a person who is going to respect you. How do you deal with it?

Respect is a learned behavior that friends in your circle should have already mastered.

Understand that people do what they know. Some people have never had a friend who has a hearing loss or any kind of disability; some people were raised in a household that diminished those who suffered a loss, and some people are just cruel and insensitive. Regardless of why people do these things, you have to understand that it is not your battle, so leave it alone, give them the boot, and move on. This is about respect. Respect cannot be taught by hollering and challenging someone. It's learned behavior—something that you simply don't have the time to teach. Got it?

POWER in your circle

Now, I mentioned earlier having power in your inner circle when speaking about being gracious and happy for others. Well, this power is just pretty much the same thing, multiplied. Now I am talking about an ongoing rotation of circle dynamics that shoot out the power of fluorescent lighting. What I mean is this… good energy among a circle is a powerful thing. Good energy can sometimes be scarce in our society as well. So, anyone who smiles daily, laughs constantly, encourages wholeheartedly, and praises genuinely has the power of one ray of light. Now, imagine how great the blended lights would be compiled of five to ten—and even up to fifty—lights.

There is no minimum or maximum number of participants within your circle; you just have to be sure they belong there. Be sure that everyone in your circle contributes to your fluorescent light's power and that you aren't feeding energy to dulled out lights. Circles of friends are comprised of many "fluorescent lights," so they should have the power of many beautiful rays of bright lights.

People in your circle should exhibit positive and tranquil energy.

In my real estate career, we regularly use the "team" metaphor when we build teams. We call it wealth-building, but it is a concept that can be used in any area of our lives. We can call it lifestyle building or even communication building. People gravitate to positive, confident energy, and this is very obvious within these real estate teams.

Within teams, if agents need questions answered, there are no shrug, impatience, or cold shoulders. We understand the energy that we have to exert and the tranquility among people that must be shared. Yes, we are also aware that we are better off learning collectively than individually, but energy is most important. We share our experiences and help each other through new experiences. Team members are chosen carefully, to be taken into a reputable team, your character has to exhibit positivity and tranquil energy.

The same gesture goes for building our circles. We emit more lighting in a circle than as a single node; standards have to be met for someone to get into your circle. This circle will be your place of leverage, and you have to be the original light of that single node.

It's pretty powerful if you think of it, I mean, no one wants to be part of a bland group of negatives where the leader can't even be positive; sounds more like a lousy doctor appointment than an inspired circle of connections. It's pretty awesome, and it will be a test of your character. However, the sooner you adopt this concept, the better equipped you will be to handle what life throws at you.

Think about it, we are hoping to acquire more influential friends. Friends who have been where we are trying to get to. Why wouldn't there be uplifting of enormous bright fluorescent light power in that? In every area of our lives, our circle should be broadening. Whether it's significant others, spiritual choir sisters, professional acquaintances, or optimistic playtime parent partners. Each of us can choose to make these connections, so we can choose who we connect with. That will determine the strength of your circle.

Push past your comfort zone
and be amazed at your growth.

We're not challenging ourselves when we surround ourselves with those who have not gotten to where we have. Nope. We are only repeating our experiences for their benefit, but there is probably not much to gain by learning from it again. No, we have to push past our comfort zones to surround ourselves with those who create amazement in us.

When we push past our comfort zones, the result is that we will later experience our own amazement by going steps further to achieve, then we know and recognize that we have grown. Here's a promise that I can make to you: the people that you connect with at the top will have this established circle, too, and it will be powerful. That is the true power of networking, a topic too large to discuss in this book. However, I've stated before that there is power in reciprocated relationships where you can give and receive, and others within your circle can do the same. You would be amazed at the number of people that still believe in and operate every day in the law of attraction. Rich people intentionally surround themselves with powerful and positive people who can, together, build power dynamics through circles.

BOUNDARIES in your circle...

What can save you from the headache of creating a terrible circle is setting and acknowledging boundaries with people. Boundaries are helpful because they establish how you want to be treated. If we're going to do this circle thing, then we have to do it right. There is no room in our circle for wishy-washy, back and forth, people—or even half-steppers. People who can't adhere to boundaries in your life simply do not belong in your circle.

You may ask people to make sure that they are facing you when you talk or to refrain from playing loud music when speaking to you. You might tell a friend, "I am glad you are riding with me, but I need you to keep quiet while I drive; then, we can talk after we arrive." Boundaries may seem a bit formal or intimidating for some people, but it's actually not. It's a great way of saying, "This is what I have been through in my life; this is what I need if you are going to be a friend."

Honestly, boundaries should be practiced in all relationships, whether you suffer from a loss or not. We simply cannot expect people to read our minds. Most importantly, if we don't allow people to know our boundaries upfront, then things will happen… something that we don't want to happen or have probably already happened and disgusted us. If we ever feel violated when we had not been clear on our boundaries, we may consider letting them off the hook because we never took the time to explain what overstepping boundaries are for us. Get it?

Yes, in all of your relationships, remember, from the start that people are not mind readers. Establishing these clear boundaries from the beginning will help us to take steps to prioritize our wants and think about the type of behavior that we will, or will not, tolerate in our lives. What irritates you? What makes a true friend? Why did your past friendships end? What have you decided that you will not tolerate? All of these questions need to be answered in order for you to set boundaries and make progress in future relationships.

Think back on past occurrences
to ensure that the past does not repeat itself.

A classic example among our population is setting boundaries about insults. Truthfully, some people really will go there if you refuse to tell them upfront. People who you want within your circle should understand what is okay and what is not. They should have a clear picture of what bothers you. You don't want to be on a ski trip in the mountains with a group of friends, being insulted because you never set boundaries with a particular friend who is just trying to have a good time. Think about it. This is the part of the book where you must think back and understand past occurrences to make progress for the future, ensuring that the past doesn't repeat itself.

This circle that you are creating is also a circle of *reciprocity*. I love that word, especially when it comes to people. In other words, I give. . . YOU give. I think that this is also a perfect example of another boundary to set with people. If there is one thing that I detest in my life, it is unbalanced and biased relationships that occur with arrogant and one-sided people. That's right, folks; we have to accurately discern when to say *yes* and say *no*. We must know that its okay to say no to people who drain us of our energy. Get ready to eliminate those who consistently pull from your circle, yet never have anything to offer. We want dependable, reliable, and trustworthy friends.

It takes time for people to truly understand
the world in which we live.

To do this, we must make clear valuable connections. This means we can tell people about ourselves, about our likes and dislikes. Making the connection with a hearing loss is not always easy, but maybe consider giving it a try at the next event that you attend. Try sharing a secret or boundary with them. For instance, just the other day, I connected with a Facebook friend. I told her about my life and hearing loss. When we met up on a Zoom page later, I asked her nicely if she could refrain from sending me FB video posts that weren't closed captioned. She has a good heart, and she means well, but she is not me, and she doesn't live through the frustration of aching to hear a video because she is so interested in the post. Some people may not understand initially, but be patient. It takes time for people to truly understand the world in which we live. Living and socializing is not as clean-cut for us as it is for others.

My point is to practice setting boundaries with acquaintances and telling them your boundaries. We must make it personal and essential. People must see how seriously we take the boundaries we set and understand that it will help us get along better. This means that we have to look at what people tend to do that we don't like; for example, the friend who wants to talk to you at 11:00 p.m., when you told her that you are enforcing a 10:00 p.m. bedtime. Or, the mother that just won't stop cleaning up your apartment when she stops by. All right, maybe you can't stop a mom for cleaning her child's apartment, but I think you get my drift, those bugaboo things that people do. But, I have to admit, overstepping boundaries doesn't have to be irritating or annoying. It can also be rude, disruptive, disrespectful, or even downright absurd.

If you truly want to live a comfortable life,
then you must learn to speak up for what you want.

Like the coworker who has to make the type of coffee she wants for the office, regardless of how others feel. If it disrupts you or annoys you, then you have a right to say, "Hey, other people would like to choose sometimes, too." Even though she is not in your circle (and hopefully she never is, being so selfish), this scenario is still coworker interaction; it is the perfect example of how people do things just because they can get away with it or because they know that no one will say anything, including you.

Did you hear what I said, that last part was for you. If you truly want to live a comfortable life, you have to learn how to speak up and ask for what you want. You have to set boundaries for what you will not tolerate. By doing this, you are learning how to make others hear you. I mean, sure you might ruffle a few feathers, or run into a few "what's the big deal" arguments, but remember, we are trying to get to the new you. If people don't understand you, then give them the boot. Be like Santa, make a list, check it twice, and find out who is naughty or nice. Who-hooo! I am killing myself in laughter right now.

But seriously, this is where you're going to have to be real and 'fess up with yourself. Tell your friend who likes to borrow money all of the time, no. Refuse to allow your family to always bring the cookout to your house. Get over friends who expect you to answer the phone every time they call. Hello, world! Life is happening all around us, and we must get this squared away to start living at our best. Besides, we're building an awesome circle right now.

Conclusion

> "The only limit to our realization of tomorrow will be our doubts of today. Let us move forward with strong and active faith."
>
> —Theodore Roosevelt
> *Physically Challenged Former POTUS*
> (President of the United States)

Imagine a life of less frustration and more relaxation; a life in which people are in tune with the way you operate. They dance and move to the beat of your drum, and they laugh and smile, enjoying your company. This is not about dictatorship, but it is about power. That is, exercising an internal power. Power to know that it's okay to expect that boundaries be respected and that it's okay to ask people to repeat things. Power to sit, unbothered by cruel remarks, power to glance throughout a large size event space and not feel intimidation, and power to allow others to intercede on your behalf, trusting that they have your best interest at heart. There does exist such a world. But you have to create it. This book has covered many important topics, but I am ending with the circle concept for a reason. It is where you will get your power.

Since I have walked you through my life experiences, and shown you how to come out on top, will you now begin building your inner circle? Trust me. Someone has done this, and it has worked. Someone has set boundaries, and it has worked. Someone has had meaningful conversations, and it has worked—someone with a hearing loss, someone just like you. You can have this life of peace and comfort, too. But it takes a vision and a desire. A vision that you can see that a better day will come through building this circle and the desire to see that day when you make these things happen.

I just want to conclude by taking a moment to recap in this last chapter. I want to help you to put it all together so that the process makes sense. I want you to return to this chapter if you need to reiterate in your life why you made the change that you did when reading this book.

Well, here's the big takeaway! This hearing loss is present in every living and breathing second of your day. The reality is that, whether you embrace it or mock it, will determine how much you are able to accomplish with it. I want a life for you in which you can be at your best every single day. Come on; we're talking about always being at our best. Always, Dominique? Never a down day? Well, understand that when we put in place certain practices, it doesn't become just a task but a way of life, so instead of expecting down days, then we are simply acquiring a new way of life.

Achieving a new way of life means that you have shaken the fear of wearing hearing aids because you know all of the advantages of them, as discussed in Chapter 3. I hope that this part of the book helped to instill courage in you, as I know that my courage makes me more optimistic every day. That is truly what I meant with the title of that chapter. Please take it as verbatim advice that you simply cannot soar, hiding in the bushes and that, in order to soar, you must be seen, which means that your hearing aids will be seen as well. Hearing aids should help you take part in a more warm and heartfelt conversation—when your circle is right. And the reality is that there are more struggles and frustration without them. So, just remember to invest in yourself by wearing your hearing aids. . . all day, every day, from dust till dawn.

Building a new way of life also means that you have shaken the fear of employers and their assumptions about you, as we learned in Chapter 5. Good employers will receive you, process your loss, and make accommodations. They will ask questions but remember not to become intimidated or hesitant. You must simply have faith that your best interest is at heart. If the process for getting an employer to understand what you need becomes too overwhelming, begin looking for better companies and employers, because there are many out there.

In Chapter 5, we also touched base on entrepreneurship and how it can work well on your behalf, if you have a hearing loss, but you must do the work.

When we learn to communicate our needs to a significant other, we have conquered a new way of living. In Chapter 6, we learned what is often most harmful to us in relationships comes from dealing with those who don't have our best interest at heart. In this case, we need to employ a system that allows us to discern others' reactions when we tell them what we need. We need to see them act for us and mediate for us, without begging them to do so. It almost has to be second nature to them. Some people practice romantic gestures in a relationship, and some don't. Some people practice compassion and thoughtfulness in a relationship, and some don't—just be sure that you are investing in someone that has enough self-care for themselves that they know the importance of caring for you. While we are on the subject of communication, remember to use your Three C's of communication that we learned in Chapter 8: compassion, confidence, and chance. Give yourself a great chance at more meaningful conversations.

Achieving a new way of life also means acknowledging bad habits. Chapter 7 talked about some of these bad habits, so now is the time to do just the opposite and exercise your good habits and try them out on your circle. If someone in your circle asks you to attend an event, make a quick decision, and live with it. If you land a new job, be sure that you never procrastinate and realize that you need your time to stay on top of your game.

Do it; live your life with self-acceptance and self-love. Go ahead and place that incredible energy out there and receive it back tenfold through the law of attraction. That is how you put it all together; you put it all into action. Where do you start, you might ask? Well, take a look at your life and ask yourself what do I need to improve on? What type of environments, events, and happenings challenge you the most? What do you think of your current skillset, and does your current job help you exercise your maximum potential? Does your significant other help you to maximize your potential? Is everyone in your circle up for the task of caring for you? Take it head-on and use the tips that I have provided here in this book.

I promise you that you are going to do fine. Just take a deep breath, breathe, and go for it.

Be honest with yourself.

In order for the coping strategies in this book to work for you, then you must first be honest with yourself. Do you land the best or worst relationships? Do people receive confidence or insecurity from you? Do you shy away at attending events, instead of planning ahead and enjoying yourself? If this book is going to work for you, then you must be honest with yourself. You want to grow, right? Well, growth is your awakening—an awakening that springs forth life in you. It is just like the first hint of sunlight shining through your window at the crack of dawn. Yet, instead, this light shining through is for the rest of your life. Once your awakening happens, it's hard to regress; in fact, I doubt that you would want to.

Chapter 4 gave us a chance to touch on our growth and glows when it comes to interaction with others. Well, now is the time to make use of that chapter. Remember, don't wear your emotions on your sleeve. When embarrassing moments happen, don't overthink it. Understand that once you are out of sight, people forget all about you and what has happened. Tomorrow is a new day. Out of sight, out of mind. And decide whether you are an introvert or extrovert. I can't stress this enough, because you must know whether you are holding yourself back from happy days or living your best life.

In Chapter 2, we learned about helping others by helping ourselves through lip reading. And that, I believe, should be a part of putting it all together as well. When we adjust to our lesser hearing senses by adopting lip-reading strategies, then we help others by helping ourselves. Yes, conversations will become a lot easier because many words (lip read) by yourself, will be picked up more naturally, and reduce work for the people you love who want you to maximize on the hearing that you do have. You will be at ease with more conversations. Indeed, you should plan to aim to master lip reading.

Challenging yourself is the key to living at your best as well. Successful people set a challenge for themselves, and they master it. I don't know of any other skill that could be as beneficial to a person of lesser hearing than to master lip reading. I mean, you could master sign language, but then you would only use it among those who know it. Lip reading is altogether different, and the ultimate language of choice for the lesser hearing. It should be pursued before sign language because it will serve us better and keep us in human connection with those who are not impacted by a hearing loss.

Everybody speaks with their lips, and words and consonants are all formed the same globally.

I absolutely had to save the best for last in summarizing Chapter 9. Your inner circle is the icing on the cake to this book. The circle is where we combine all that we have learned in this book. Most importantly, we create better surroundings. Better friends. Better experiences. Better life. Remember that everyone in your circle should exhibit respect (towards others), power (in what they bring to the table), and understand your boundaries (so that you can be comfortable and trust them). This circle grows your life when you start with the people that you trust, and you go outward.

In everything that you do in life, start with the people that you trust. Start with your circle. Even if you are simply going to get a tire changed, start with your circle. Trying a new hairstyle and looking for a new stylist? Start with your circle. Many vindictive people get a thrill out of steering people the wrong way, so why ask for their help when you have your trusted circle?

As lesser hearing people, we have to step up and claim the situation that God gave us. We have to dare to dream of the limitless sky, even if that means a few bumps in the road to get there. There is nothing more rewarding than reaching your potential and watching yourself excel at something. Even in being lesser hearing, there is still something that each of us is gifted with, so get busy. Put it all together. Rejoice in the fact that you know that you are not alone and that you have learned some essential steps to help you on your way. This is your awakening. Your time to...

Awaken to a better day.

Awaken to less frustration.

Awaken to more self-acceptance.

Awaken to more self-awareness.

Awaken to increased self-confidence.

Awaken to being just as good as the next person, if not better.

Until next time!

Endnotes

Chapter 1

1. Reese, 2013 www.mintpressnews.com/amid-discrimination-deaf-americans-still-struggle-to-find-acceptance/164582/

2. NIH article www.ncbi.nlm.nih.gov/pmc/articles/PMC3983202/

3. WebMD www.webmd.com/parenting/help-for-parents-hearing-impaired-children#1

4. Medical News Today article https://www.medicalnewstoday.com/articles/249285

Chapter 2

1. Hearing Loss: Determining eligibility for social security benefits www.ncbi.nlm.nih.gov/books/NBK207836/

2. What is lipreading? www.hearinglink.org/living/lipreading-communicating/what-is-lipreading/

3. What is lipreading? www.hearinglink.org/living/lipreading-communicating/what-is-lipreading/ (repeat reference used)

4. 10 Benefits of Reading: www.lifehack.org/articles/lifestyle/10-benefits-reading-whyyou-should-read-everyday.html

5. Simmons, R. (2014). Success Through Stillness: Meditation Made Simple. Penguin Random House.

Chapter 3

1. Hearing Solutions 2018: www.hearingsolutionsok.com/2018/06/20/the-hearing-aidfashion-statement/

2. National Association of the Deaf: www.nad.org/resources/technology/caption-access-in-movie-theaters/

3. Ashley Derrington, Hearing Like Me: www.hearinglikeme.com/top-benefits-of-hiring-deaf-andhard-of-hearing-people/

4. Healthy Hearing: www.healthyhearing.com/report/52437-The-complex-link-between-depression-and-hearing-loss

5. (2016). The Benefits of Speech Therapy in Your Child's Development. Pedia Plex Blog. https://pediaplex.net/blog/the-benefits-of-speech-therapy-in-your-childs-development/

6. Gendry, S. (2016). Help for Depression: Laugh to Activate Happy Feelings. Laughter Online University. https://www.laughteronlineuniversity.com/help-for-depression/

7. Sanchez, G. (2016). Why People Love Great Visuals, Based on Science. https://piktochart.com/blog/why-people-love-great-visuals-science/

Section II Lead Page

1. Burchard, B. (2017). High Performance Habits: How Extraordinary People Become That Way. Hay House, Inc.

Chapter 5

1. Schumer, L. (2019). How to Disclose a Disability to an Employer. New York Times. https://www.nytimes.com/2019/07/10/smarter-living/disclose-disability-work-employer-rights.html

2. Higher Education Recruitment Consortium . (2017). Disclosing Disability to An Employer: Why to- When to- How to. https://www.hercjobs.org/disclosing-disability-to-an-employer-why-to-when-to-how-to/

Chapter 6

1. Tine Tjørnhøj-Thomsen and Hans Henrik Philipsen. 2018. *Hearing Loss as a Social Problem: A Study of Hearing-impaired Spouses and Their Hearing Partners.* 19 Feb 2019. <https://www.hearingreview.com/hearing-loss/patient-care/hearing-loss-as-a-social-problem

2. Tine Tjørnhøj-Thomsen and Hans Henrik Philipsen. 2018. *Hearing Loss as a Social Problem: A Study of Hearing-impaired Spouses and Their Hearing Partners.* 19 Feb 2019. <https://www.hearingreview.com/hearing-loss/patient-care/hearing-loss-as-a-social-problem (repeat reference)

3. Carlson, R. (1997). *Don't sweat the small stuff-- and it's all small stuff: Simple ways to keep the little things from taking over your life.* New York: Hyperion.

4. D. Gilbert, S. Fiske & G. Lindsey (Eds.), Handbook of social psychology (4h ed.), Vol. 2. (pp. 41-88). Boston: McGraw-Hill

5. Harvey, S. (2013). Straight Talk. No Chaser. Swindon: Milkway Media.

6. Boothman, N. (2000). How To Make People Like You in 90 Seconds or Less. New York: Workmen Publishing.

7. Tine Tjørnhøj-Thomsen and Hans Henrik Philipsen. 2018. *Hearing Loss as a Social Problem: A Study of Hearing-impaired Spouses and Their Hearing Partners.* 19 Feb 2019. <https://www.hearingreview.com/hearing-loss/patient-care/hearing-loss-as-a-social-problem>

Chapter 7

1. https://en.m.wikipedia.org/wiki/Procrastination Visual integer line https://www.google.com/searchq=number+line+with+negative+and+positive&rlz=1C9BKJA_enUS779US779&oq=number+line+with+negative+and+positive&aqs=chro me..69i57j0l3.6691j0j7&hl=en-US&sourceid=chrome-mobile&ie=UTF-8#imgrc=Ogty4Qiv5F6lGM

Chapter 8

1. University of Missouri-Columbia. "People who rely on their intuition are, at times, less likely to cheat." ScienceDaily. ScienceDaily, 24 November 2015. <www.sciencedaily.com/releases/2015/11/151124143502.htm>.

www.ingramcontent.com/pod-product-compliance
Lightning Source LLC
LaVergne TN
LVHW021800060526
838201LV00058B/3179